# IT'S ALL ABOUT PEOPLE SKILLS

# IT'S ALL ABOUT PEOPLE SKILLS

## Surviving Challenges in the Classroom

JERRY BOYLE

ROWMAN & LITTLEFIELD EDUCATION

*A division of*
ROWMAN & LITTLEFIELD PUBLISHERS, INC.
Lanham • New York • Toronto • Plymouth, UK

Published by Rowman & Littlefield Education
A division of Rowman & Littlefield Publishers, Inc.
A wholly owned subsidiary of The Rowman & Littlefield Publishing Group, Inc.
4501 Forbes Boulevard, Suite 200, Lanham, Maryland 20706
http://www.rowmaneducation.com

Estover Road, Plymouth PL6 7PY, United Kingdom

Copyright © 2012 by Jerry Boyle

*All rights reserved.* No part of this book may be reproduced in any form or by any electronic or mechanical means, including information storage and retrieval systems, without written permission from the publisher, except by a reviewer who may quote passages in a review.

British Library Cataloguing in Publication Information Available

**Library of Congress Cataloging-in-Publication Data**

Boyle, Jerry, 1936-
 It's all about people skills : surviving challenges in the classroom / Jerry Boyle.
   p. cm.
 Includes index.
 ISBN 978-1-61048-609-5 (cloth : alk. paper) — ISBN 978-1-61048-610-1 (pbk. : alk. paper) — ISBN 978-1-61048-611-8 (ebook)
 1. Effective teaching.  2. Classroom environment.  3. Classroom management.  4. Communication in education.  I. Title.
 LB1025.3.B696 2012
 371.102—dc23                                                                2011040603

∞™ The paper used in this publication meets the minimum requirements of American National Standard for Information Sciences—Permanence of Paper for Printed Library Materials, ANSI/NISO Z39.48-1992.

Printed in the United States of America

# CONTENTS

| | | |
|---|---|---|
| Foreword | | vii |
| Introduction | | xi |
| 1 | The Nature of Effective Teaching | 1 |
| 2 | People Skills: Foundation of Effective Teaching | 13 |
| 3 | Managing to Teach: Print-to-Practice Strategies | 25 |
| 4 | The Classroom Management Plan: Bringing It All Together | 35 |
| 5 | The Home-School Connection | 43 |
| 6 | Using Surveys | 49 |
| 7 | Meeting the Challenge | 57 |
| 8 | Engaging Students in Learning | 67 |
| 9 | Creating a Positive School Culture | 75 |
| 10 | The Effect of Poverty on Teaching and Learning | 81 |
| 11 | Time for Reflection: Putting Your Thoughts into Writing | 87 |
| 12 | Summary and Conclusion | 93 |
| Index | | 99 |
| About the Author | | 101 |
| Acknowledgments | | 103 |

This book is dedicated to my grandson, Tyler,
who is at the beginning of his educational journey.

# FOREWORD

> A child miseducated is a child lost.
>
> —John F. Kennedy

Without question, the most important profession is that of a teacher. All the other professions are first taught by teachers, and without teachers we would have no other professions. Moreover, research tells us that the single most important factor in the success of our children is the classroom teacher. This research also shows that two years of a great teacher will accelerate a student's learning trajectory, whereas two bad teachers in a row will dramatically harm this trajectory and the harm cannot be made up. This book provides a good context for the importance of a teacher and provides a breakdown of those skills needed to be a great teacher.

> The mediocre teacher tells. The good teacher explains. The superior teacher demonstrates. The great teacher inspires.
>
> —Arthur Ward

As the quote above suggests, becoming a teacher is more than learning a set of skills that allows you to transmit knowledge to students. It is more! Yes, great teachers must have the necessary skills needed to teach, but they also must have the interpersonal skills to motivate and inspire their students. They must be creative and find ways to meet the different learning needs of their students. In addition, they must have great assessment skills and the ability to differentiate instruction. Finally, they must be adroit at managing the classroom and making it an environment that encourages learning.

This book provides a balanced view of teaching and a clear set of skills needed by all good teachers. At the same time, there is an emphasis on those interpersonal skills needed to inspire the students of tomorrow. Finally, Dr. Boyle does a good job of helping prospective teachers understand the complex interdependency of the many teaching and interdisciplinary skills that a teacher must embrace in order to be a truly great teacher who can inspire!

> It is the supreme art of the teacher to awaken joy in creative expression and knowledge.
>
> —Albert Einstein

Teaching is an interactive partnership with your students. It is not about you pouring knowledge into the empty vessels of your students. Rather, you are engaging with your students as collaborative colearners to understand the concepts you are trying to impart to your students. Often this involves the teacher tapping into the internal understandings of the students and helping them use the information they have in a new and unique way that expands their knowledge. At other times, you as a teacher see a concept from your students' point of view and find that you now have a new understanding that expands your views. Good teachers teach and great teachers learn while they are teaching.

> The dream begins with a teacher who believes in you, who tugs and pushes and leads you to the next plateau, sometimes poking you with a sharp stick called truth.
>
> —Dan Rather

As a teacher, it is important that you believe in your students and find the best in every student. It is equally important that you help them see the facts and that you don't accept information or responses that are not consistent with the facts in an attempt to be supportive of your students. Students need to know the facts, they need to know when they need to work harder on a project, and they need to to understand when they don't have a right answer. This must be completed in a way that empowers students and helps them understand that they have the skills to "get it right." The interpersonal skills talked about in this book will help you achieve that balance between being supportive and at the same time asking your students to strive for more.

> Those who can, do; those who can't, teach.
>
> —George Bernard Shaw

Unfortunately, this statement suggests that people who have failed or would be failures in the "real world" decide to become teachers. Nothing could be further from the truth, and as you work on your teaching skills you are going to find out just how challenging this profession is to master. You will hear other statements like Shaw's, and it is important for you to help people see the truth and understand how important the job of a teacher is to society. The skills you learn from reading this book will help you develop a repertoire of skills to be a great teacher who can inspire your students. Your success will help people understand the folly of this statement and help change the minds of those who are not supportive of our profession.

★★★

As my last thought: This is what teaching and being a teacher is all about. As a teacher, you will have a profound impact on the students you teach. Your impact doesn't stop with the children you teach; it will echo through generations. This is a great service, and you will find it an incredibly rewarding experience. Think about the great teachers you had and how they taught you. How does this impact how you interact with others? In fact, I will bet that many of you who are reading this book are pursuing a career in teaching because you had a great teacher. As I said, the impact of a great teacher is profound, and this impact reverberates through generations. I wish you the best as you pursue this career, and I think you will find this an excellent book to help you achieve your goals.

Lawrence J. Johnson, PhD
Dean and Professor
College of Education, Criminal Justice, and Human Services
University of Cincinnati

# INTRODUCTION

Teaching is an essential profession. Who among us has not had the experience of a teacher in their lives? If one is educated, it is all but guaranteed that a teacher was a part of that process. Teaching makes all other professions possible.

More than ever before in the history of our country, the level of education makes the difference between those who will benefit from our economy and those who will struggle. Education is the profession that is shaping the future of our great country.

Teaching is difficult and is increasingly becoming a more demanding job. Students bring enormous challenges into the school. Schools do not create these problems but must find solutions to them. Teachers are instrumental in solving these problems. The kinds and numbers of challenges students are bringing into schools today are becoming more serious, frequent, and complex in nature. The media constantly reminds us of this phenomenon.

It is a matter of practice for teachers to work long hours each day at school. After a long day at school, working at home on school-related matters, such as lesson planning for the next day or grading student work, is not unusual.

The goal of every teacher is to achieve results with his or her students, including those students who create the biggest challenges. There is no doubt in the minds of many that teachers are America's greatest heroes! Teachers are education's greatest asset.

There needs to be a rebirth of teaching's being treated as a highly respected profession. Good teachers need to be recognized and supported for their excellence in the classroom. Poorly performing teachers need to be dismissed, as their influence on students can be significant and long lasting.

The nature of teaching and the expectations of teachers have been in constant change throughout the history of our country. During early American colonial days, ministers and housewives did the teaching. Later in the same period of American history, "dame" schools appeared, with the purpose of educating women. Subsequently, Latin schools opened, offering an educational opportunity for boys.

During the 1800s, significant changes took place in the teaching profession. Colonial states required towns having more than five hundred families to establish a high school. In the 1840s, school systems were created. There was also an increase in teacher training and pay. In 1857, the National Teachers Association was created; it was the largest labor union in the country. In most states at the time, teachers needed to take a test leading to certification that licensed them to teach.

During the 1900s, teaching became a more desirable profession. Improving teaching to serve the educational needs of students in a rapidly changing society became a national priority. During this same time period, more males entered the teaching profession.

Today teaching has moved into an age of technology, which includes the use of the Internet and computers. The result of these innovations has dramatically changed what we teach and how we teach in classrooms. At the same time, these innovations have created new and exciting learning opportunities for students of all ages and grade levels. These innovations also present challenges to teachers, students, and parents.

Currently, as in the past, good teachers are in demand. Good teachers make good schools. Harry Wong, accomplished author and motivational speaker, makes it clear that "it's people, not programs" that impact student achievement.

The purpose of this book is to inform and educate the reader. It is written as a resource for current and future use. It has been designed to serve the needs of experienced educators as well as those new to the field of education.

This book focuses on two important components involved in teaching. The first is interpersonal or people skills, essential to successful teaching. The second is instructional strategies.

Simply stated, this book is about *who* the teacher is (people skills) and *what* the teacher does in the classroom (instructional strategies). The importance of these two components cannot be overstated, as they are at the core of successful teaching. The question is, which of the two is more important? Research statistics are available showing that many teachers leave the profession during their first three to five years in the classroom. One reason for this is inadequate classroom management skills.

# CHAPTER REVIEWS

*Chapter 1*

Chapter 1 presents an overview of the nature of effective teaching, identifying roles and responsibilities involved. Differences between academic skills and people skills are discussed.

Key concepts in this chapter include the following:

- The importance of planning for teaching
- The role that people skills play in teaching
- Engaging students in the learning process
- Profile of a "good" teacher

*Chapter 2*

Chapter 2 asks the readers to take a look at themselves in terms of their people or interpersonal skills. The chapter is designed with a hands-on approach, providing a self-assessment activity. "Reflection" is the key concept.

*Chapter 3*

Being effective in the classroom depends upon a sound instructional program and the skills needed to successfully implement it.

Two key concepts are the focus in chapter 3:

- "Print to Practice" strategies for successful teaching
- A toolbox of skills needed to support successful teaching

*Chapter 4*

A classroom management plan provides the "road map for teaching." This road map guides the development of the instructional program. Teaching can be compared to driving a car—both need direction! Usually, one would not begin driving without having a destination in mind and a way to get there. Teaching, like driving, must have a destination, or goals, in mind. The way to reach these goals is through the use of an effective classroom management plan. It is the foundation of the planning process. This chapter focuses on creating an effective classroom management plan.

*Chapter 5*

"It takes a village to raise a child"—and it takes a team to educate a child. The team includes the child, teachers, parents, and others who are part of the educational setting. Parental involvement in their child's schooling is essential if the child is to reach his or her highest level of achievement. Suggestions for creating a meaningful home-school connection are discussed in this chapter.

Key concept: The importance of school and home working together is a major priority and cannot be overstated.

*Chapter 6*

Surveys provide data. Surveys also generate opinions. Most important is how the data and opinions obtained are used. Chapter 6 looks at the nature and purpose of surveys. A sample educational survey related to traits of an effective teacher is presented and analyzed.

*Chapter 7*

Surviving in the classroom depends on how successfully teachers meet the challenges they encounter on a regular basis. These challenges range from simple to complex in nature. Some are less serious—some are very serious. Dealing with these challenges is a learning process for teachers as well as for all school personnel. Appropriate people skills are an essential part of this process. This chapter addresses some of these classroom challenges.

*Chapter 8*

Teachers teach—students learn! That is the expectation. The responsibility of the teacher is to "engage students in their own learning." If students are not successfully engaged in learning, the level of achievement becomes questionable. Engaging students does not happen automatically. It is linked to the relevance of both the content and delivery of instruction. Developing a collaborative teaching-learning environment in the classroom is key to engaging students. Cooperative learning is one example of collaboration that works in many classrooms if properly planned, structured, and monitored by the teacher.

*Chapter 9*

Each of us has a personality. It defines who we are and how we relate to others. Our personality can be positive or negative in nature. Others can identify our personality as they interact with us. Not only do individuals have a personality, schools also have a personality. School personality is referred to as the school's *climate*, better known as the climate that exists within the school. Traits, or characteristics, of a positive school culture are identified.

*Chapter 10*

Children living in poverty attend many of our nation's schools. More attend urban schools than other type of schools. Poverty puts many students at risk both academically and socially. Poverty also contributes to diversity in the classroom. Poverty does have an effect on teaching and learning. Warning signs exist that may indicate that a student is at risk. Teachers must recognize these warning signs and provide opportunities for these students in the instructional program, as well as in the social environment in the classroom.

*Chapter 11*

Reflection refers to how we evaluate our thinking about particular issues relevant to our lives. This can include professional as well as social-behavioral issues. This chapter provides an opportunity for the reader to *reflect* upon the content of this book. Putting reflections into *writing* can, in many instances, impact their significance by seeing what you were thinking!

*Chapter 12*

This chapter presents some of the highlights of the book.

The conclusion the reader should come to is an understanding of two components that significantly impact successful teaching. One is the interpersonal or people skills needed to survive in the classroom. The other is the use of effective teaching strategies that support a strong instructional program. Neither component stands alone. Both are needed to successfully survive in the classroom.

The next step is to continue to be a lifelong learner. Participating in appropriate professional development programs, college courses, and/or activities offers one way to achieve this goal.

# 1

# THE NATURE OF EFFECTIVE TEACHING

> The mediocre teacher tells. The good teacher explains. The superior teacher demonstrates. The great teacher inspires.
>
> —William A. Ward, American scholar, author, editor, and teacher

Over the years there have been many books written with the purpose of identifying, as well as defining, the effective teacher and good teaching. Many of these books focused on theory. This is not to say that theory is unimportant in defining what makes a teacher effective. However, theory cannot do the job alone.

The first intent of this book is to present strategies, or best practices, to support effective teaching. A second intent is to identify the specific people skills, also referred to as interpersonal skills, essential to becoming a successful teacher. A self-evaluation scale is included for the reader to use. A third intent is to discuss how to write a meaningful classroom management plan. A fourth intent is to analyze the use of educational surveys. The final intent is to review the challenges that teachers meet in today's classrooms.

The reader will be able to take much of the information presented in this book from print to practice, therefore making it a hands-on approach. The focus is on *who* the teacher is and *what* the teacher does in the classroom.

## ABOUT TEACHERS

It goes without saying that most of us have been influenced by a teacher sometime during our life. Being a teacher is one of the most important careers in our society. Teachers provide knowledge, discipline, and a role model for students.

Children from a very young age until their late teenage years spend most of their waking hours each day in school. Kids leave home early in the morning and usually do not get home until mid- or late afternoon. This allows them only a few hours to spend time with family.

Teachers have many important responsibilities, including acting *in loco parentis*—or taking the place of parents—while students are under their care. The influence teachers have on students of all ages is far-reaching and in many cases long-lasting. Teachers need to be academically prepared and demonstrate a wide range of people or interpersonal skills. Teachers regularly interact with students, parents, other staff members, administrators, and often with community members.

## THE TEACHER AND THE JOB

Teaching is a service profession. Teachers make hundreds of decisions daily which range from simple to complex. Each week, approximately nine to ten months a year, the teacher performs in the classroom. Teachers take to the stage in front of an audience that is not always cooperative, friendly, receptive, or interested in being present. Teachers do this six to seven hours a day, five days a week, forty-plus weeks each school year.

In order to be successful, teachers must exhibit a caring attitude and be both motivated and motivating at all times. They must demonstrate a high level of academic ability, while at the same time have an awareness of the needs of each and every student for whom they are responsible.

Before teachers take the stage for a day of performing, it is a prerequisite that they spend time preparing their script, or lessons to be taught. Good lesson planning is essential for successful teaching.

Planning for teaching involves, but is not limited to, the following guidelines:

- Lessons need to be aligned to academic standards.
- Lessons need to show relevance.
- Lessons need to allow for differences in student learning levels.

- Lessons need to allow for student participation.
- Lessons need to allow for cultural diversity.
- Lessons need to show a variety of teaching methods and presentation styles.
- Lessons need to be well written, with objectives clearly stated.

Creating effective lesson plans requires skill on the part of the classroom teacher. Poorly written lesson plans can create a disappointing learning experience. The importance of well-written lesson plans cannot be overstated. It is a skill required of every teacher. Once the lesson plans are written, it is time for the show to begin—time for teaching!

People skills become part of the process as lesson plans are presented. Once the teacher takes the stage, engaging the students' attention is the next step. At this time, lesson plans come alive! How successful they are depends on the quality of the plans themselves and the effectiveness of the teacher while executing them. This is show time.

Well-written lesson plans are at the core of effective teaching. Lesson plans reflect the beginning of the teaching cycle. Bigger challenges are still to come! Lesson plans serve as a valuable resource for effective teaching. Many teachers possess the skills needed to create well-written lesson plans. However, it is possible for a teacher to create well-written lesson plans but subsequently not be able to present an effective lesson using those plans. Making lesson plans come alive, as well as making them effective, is a major responsibility of every teacher.

The question is, how do you know *when* a teacher is effective? It is sometimes easier to identify those behaviors that make a teacher less than effective or totally ineffective. The teacher is the most important influence on student achievement. The teacher *is* curriculum.

## THE QUALITY FACTOR

It would be impossible to develop a list of all the skills, abilities, and traits that contribute to making a teacher effective. However, it is possible to create a starting point.

High-performing teachers share several classroom management skills as well as certain teaching methods and techniques. Additionally, high-performing teachers have a high level of student engagement skills. High-performing teachers bring their personality to the classroom, which is focused on students. Their personality can be described as caring.

## AN EXERCISE IN SELF-ASSESSMENT

Several strategies that support effective teaching will be presented. People skills necessary to be an effective teacher will also be identified. A self-evaluation scale is available for use by the reader. This scale will provide you with an opportunity to place yourself somewhere between the lower end, or *Needs Improvement*, and the higher end, or *Very Effective*.

For those readers who are not currently teaching, placement on the evaluation scale will reflect where you feel you would like to be if you were teaching. Using this scale is, of course, optional. As stated, its purpose is to be used as a self-evaluative instrument. If you choose to use this instrument, your self-ratings will help describe your level of success in the classroom.

We begin our presentation by identifying those skills that contribute to making a teacher effective. Many relate to interpersonal skills or *people skills*. As mentioned, teaching is a service profession, and success in providing this service depends on interpersonal skills.

## ACADEMICS + PEOPLE SKILLS

Being a service profession, teaching includes both people skills and academic skills. Teachers can be highly competent in terms of academic preparation. They can also be highly proficient in writing effective lesson plans, which obviously is an academic skill.

Academic preparation is a major as well as a required part of what makes a teacher effective. However, taking academic competency and training into the classroom requires people skills in order to be successful. The first three to five years of teaching can be benchmark years in determining if one has what it takes to be successful.

An individual teacher may have acquired a substantial amount of subject matter, yet be unable to design and use relevant instructional methods to enhance student learning due a lack of pedagogical skills. Conversely, an individual teacher may possess the necessary pedagogical skills, yet have limited subject-matter knowledge—which can also result in ineffective teaching.

These scenarios indicate that it is impossible to be an effective teacher without being competent in both subject-matter knowledge and pedagogical skills. Consequently, subject-matter knowledge remains a necessary prerequisite for effective teaching, but not the sole determinant. (Sean T. Bulger, *Journal of Effective Teaching*, 5, no. 2, 2002)

## SOME FACTS WORTH CONSIDERING

In Chicago (Rossi, 2005), 1,116 nontenured teachers struggling to control their classrooms were nonrenewed. Nearly half of these teachers had problems with classroom management, and the other half struggled with instructional issues according to reasons indicated by principals:

- Classroom management problems, 55 percent
- Ineffective instruction, 46 percent
- Lack of responsibility, 38 percent
- Poor communication with parents/staff, 26 percent
- Attitude/lack of cooperation, 20 percent

The early years of teaching provide time for teachers to decide if teaching is what they want to do or what they are able to do. Success during these early years is based not only upon academic competency but upon one's people skills in the classroom as well.

Studies have shown that teachers leave their profession in far greater numbers based upon their lack of people skills as they relate to working effectively with students. Fewer teachers leave teaching because of a lack of academic preparation. Research estimates that approximately 50 percent of teachers leave during the first three to five years of their career. A major cause is their inability to manage student behavior in their classroom.

Can people skills be improved? The answer to that question is yes—given appropriate time and support. The next and most important question is how.

The first step is for teachers to identify and admit the nature of their problem. The second, and equally important, step is their willingness to seek continuing support and mentoring.

Step 2 can be more difficult than step 1. Step 1 calls upon the wisdom and strength of teachers to identify and admit to the problems they are experiencing. Unfortunately, in certain situations, the teachers do not understand they have problems! Often they claim the problems rest with their students, not with them, or with other situations within the school environment.

This is where step 2 comes into play. Being willing to seek and accept support and mentoring from others can provide the pathway to creating possibilities for improving people skills. It involves change, and that is sometimes a very difficult process.

Opportunities are available for teachers to improve their academic skills. These opportunities include taking additional college work and/or professional development activities. Opportunities are also available for teachers to improve their people skills. The decision to take advantage of these opportunities must be made by the teacher. It can be easier to determine what additional college or professional development work is necessary to improve academic skills than to recognize what support is needed to improve people skills.

This book presents strategies to support effective teaching, as well as identifying certain people skills that contribute to making a teacher effective.

## TO BE OR NOT TO BE . . . A TEACHER

There are students who decide as early as high school to become teachers. At this point, a counselor should guide these students to pursue or not pursue that goal, based upon their individual qualifications at the time.

Traditionally, college students in teacher-training programs do not have extensive opportunities to use their people skills in the classroom until later years in the program. In certain situations, students do have a limited exposure sooner, but it is usually not significant enough to make a real difference in terms of effectively managing student behavior.

The student teaching experience does, however, provide an opportunity for teachers-in-training to understand the importance of managing student behavior in the classroom. The greatest concern often voiced by student teachers is managing behavior in their classrooms. Much less concern has to do with their perceived lack of academic preparation or content knowledge.

The importance of teachers' interpersonal or people skills in the classroom cannot be overstated in terms of their being successful.

## THE NATURE OF TEACHING: WHAT DOES IT REALLY INVOLVE?

The nature of teaching relates directly to what makes a good teacher. The effectiveness of the teacher creates successful teaching. Good teaching and good teachers go hand in hand.

An article by Richard Leblanc appearing in *The Teaching Professor* (June–July 1998) titled "Good Teaching: The Top Ten Commandments" listed the following:

> 1. Good teaching is as much about passion as it is about reason. It's about not only motivating students to learn, but teaching them how

to learn, and doing so in a manner that is relevant, meaningful, and memorable.
2. Good teaching is about substance and treating students as consumers of knowledge.
3. Good teaching is about listening, questioning, being responsive, and remembering that each student and class is different. It's about pushing students to excel while at the same time being human.
4. Good teaching is not always about having a fixed agenda and being rigid, but being flexible, fluid, experimenting, and having the confidence to react and adjust to changing circumstances.
5. Good teaching is about style. Should good teaching be entertaining? You bet! Good teachers work the room and every student in it.
6. This is very important—good teaching is about humor. It's about ... not taking yourself too seriously ... letting students learn in a more relaxed atmosphere.
7. Good teaching is about caring, nurturing, and developing minds and talents. It's about devoting time to every student.
8. Good teaching is supported by strong and visionary leadership. Good teaching is continually reinforced by an overarching vision that transcends the entire organization and is reflected in what is said, but more importantly in what is done.
9. Good teaching is about mentoring between senior and junior faculty and about teamwork.
10. At the end of the day, good teaching is about having fun, experiencing pleasure and intrinsic rewards.

This article identifies ten important requisites involved in the nature of teaching. Including this article on a school faculty meeting agenda should create an interesting discussion. The responses should be noteworthy!

## ENGAGING STUDENTS IN THE CLASSROOM

Intrinsic to the nature of teaching is the problem of student, or client, cooperation. The student must be willing to learn what the teacher is teaching. Unless this intended learning takes place, the teacher is understood as having failed. (David Cohen, "On the Nature of Teaching and Teacher Education," *Journal of Teacher Education*, 1988, p. 55)

Teachers face this situation every day in the classroom. Even though the teacher is academically prepared and possesses adequate people skills, engaging students actively in the learning process is not guaranteed.

There could be one or many reasons why students are not engaged. Let's look at some of those potential reasons.

Could the problem be related to teacher personality? Has the teacher employed ineffective methods or techniques in his or her presentation? Has the teacher failed to ask thought-provoking questions to capture student interest? Are lesson objectives unclear? Can the problem be as simple as poorly written lesson plans? Has no attempt been made to involve the students in planning lessons? Has the teacher failed to provide for student participation during the lesson presentation?

The focus here is related to active or passive learning on the part of the students. A final consideration of the problem should relate to the classroom management skills of the teacher.

These are just a few of the considerations to be made by teachers if engaging students is a problem. Each of these considerations should be carefully reviewed, evaluated, and reflected upon.

Student engagement in the learning process is at the core of a successful classroom management plan. Engaging students brings about a team effort in the classroom between the teacher and students. The key word here is *team*!

An often-overlooked technique is taking time periodically to let your students know how they are progressing. Learning can be better understood by students if they are aware of their progress or lack of it.

A feel-good approach on the part of the teacher would be to ask students how they feel they are progressing. This approach could lead to some meaningful and beneficial outcomes, including positive responses from students. More importantly, it will create an opportunity for dialogue between teacher and students.

Creating a dialogue gives the teacher an opportunity to show how he or she cares about students. The classroom then will take on an atmosphere of being student centered. Dialogue can also enhance an effective classroom management plan.

## GOOD TEACHERS REWARD STUDENT ACHIEVEMENT WITH PRAISE

Most individuals appreciate being noticed for their achievements. This includes students of all ages. Praising students on their achievement will instill a feeling of competence, while encouraging them at the same time. Rewarding students, when appropriate, will heighten the probability that these students will retain the material or repeat the good behavior involved.

Praise, used effectively and sincerely, is a powerful tool to be used in the classroom. It can also be an important part of an effective classroom management plan. The key here is for the teacher to determine when and how often to use praise. Like any successful teaching tool, it can be used ineffectively and hence have little or no effect in terms of the intended outcome.

## GOOD TEACHERS KNOW THEIR SUBJECT MATTER

Good teachers not only know their subject matter well but they stay current with it. They consider professional development as an integral part of their job, as well as participating in other learning opportunities. Good teachers understand that they do not know everything! They make it a practice to learn from others—including the students. Good teachers are lifelong learners.

## GOOD TEACHERS USE QUESTIONING AS AN IMPORTANT TEACHING STRATEGY

Two major purposes for using questioning as a teaching strategy are: one, it focuses on student participation in the learning process, and two, it serves as a regular assessment tool.

Good teachers possess the skills necessary to create meaningful questions and know when and how frequently to use them during instruction.

## GOOD TEACHERS ARE GOOD COMMUNICATORS AND GOOD LISTENERS

Communication skills are extremely important in teaching. This also includes being a culturally competent communicator, because of the increasing student diversity that exists in today's classrooms. Knowing subject matter alone is not enough.

Effective communication is a requisite for successful teaching. Students rely on clarity as the lesson is presented by the teacher. If students do not understand what is being taught, it goes without saying that learning will be put seriously at risk.

Observing a teacher with poor communication skills is not uncommon in some of our classrooms. An important part of communication is the ability to be a good listener. Good teachers develop effective listening skills. Communication involves both speaking and listening.

## GOOD TEACHERS HAVE TIME MANAGEMENT SKILLS

Good teachers use time wisely. Teaching should not allow for time that is not planned well or is random in nature. Effective lesson plans need to be well organized, with a focus on time management related to both teaching and learning. Time wasted in the classroom can never be recaptured! Every minute counts. The proper use of time is necessary, but this does not mean that achieving that goal should create a tense atmosphere in the classroom. Learning takes place in a more relaxed atmosphere and one that is nonthreatening.

## GOOD TEACHERS HAVE A SENSE OF HUMOR AND LET IT SHOW

Having and demonstrating a sense of humor in the classroom is an essential tool for successful teaching. Teaching and learning are to be taken seriously. However, humor and wit on the part of the teacher creates a more relaxed atmosphere in the classroom. The absence of humor leads to a more rigid environment in the classroom. Learning needs to be fun and enjoyable.

## GOOD TEACHERS HAVE A FAIR ATTITUDE

Being fair is one of the hallmarks of an effective teacher. Everyone wants to be treated fairly—in and out of the classroom. Students identify easily with a teacher who treats them fairly on a regular basis. Being fair is another essential tool needed for success in the classroom. All teachers need to reflect on their fairness in dealing with students. How many times has the statement been made by students "My teacher is unfair"? True or not, it is the perception that counts!

## GOOD TEACHERS ARE TEAM PLAYERS

Teaching cannot exist in a vacuum. Most teachers have a lot to offer to students as well as to their colleagues. The saying "It takes a village to raise a child" applies to educating a child as well. A focus on teaming and team-based classrooms has evolved in the past few decades in education. Working and sharing expertise between and among teachers has produced positive results in terms of improving student achievement. The day is gone when teachers work in isolation in their own classrooms.

## GOOD TEACHERS ARE COMPETENT IN THE USE OF TECHNOLOGY IN THE CLASSROOM

One of the most significant changes in today's classroom is the introduction and use of various types of technology aimed at enhancing teaching and learning. Adapting to the use of technology and methods associated with its use has not been a smooth or easy transition for many teachers. The bottom line is that technology in today's classroom is here to stay and will become more a part of the teaching/learning process on a regular basis. Teachers, experienced or less experienced, must meet this challenge.

## GOOD TEACHERS ARE APPROACHABLE

This is one more tool necessary for teachers to be successful in the classroom. Students must not only feel their teachers are fair, have a sense of humor, are caring, and are competent in their subject matter but they must feel their teachers are approachable. Teachers being approachable is very important to students. It creates a meaningful relationship between students and teachers.

## GOOD TEACHERS HAVE PATIENCE

Teachers lacking patience will find it difficult to survive for a long period of time in the classroom. It goes without saying that one's patience can be put to the test. However, the teacher must meet this challenge and continue to demonstrate the patience needed to keep the situation under control.

Good teachers have patience and practice this skill on a regular basis. Patient teachers are great teachers!

Good teachers do not allow every disturbance in the classroom to get out of hand. Sometimes it is more productive to let some minor situations go unnoticed rather than calling attention to them and running the risk of escalating the problem. Patience involves remaining calm when the circumstances become trying. Keeping a cool temperament is a valuable skill practiced by successful teachers.

## GOOD TEACHERS ARE ABOUT MORE THAN STANDARDIZED TEST SCORES

Student learning is undoubtedly the most appropriate measure of teacher quality, but to assume that standardized test scores in reading and math are indicative of what children should learn in school represents an overly simplistic vision. (Karen Zumwalt, "Teacher Quality Can't Be Measured by Scores Alone," Columbia University Teachers College, p. 211)

In addition to teaching children to read and do math, good teachers provide an environment where students feel safe and are actively engaged in their own learning and where high expectations are held for every child.

## DISCUSSION QUESTIONS

1. What is the significance of the following concept: "The teacher *is* the curriculum"?
2. Identify some possible strategies you might use is assisting other teachers to improve their people skills.
3. In practice, what does the concept *in loco parentis* mean for the classroom teacher?
4. List five people skills you believe you possess that will contribute to success in managing students in the classroom.
5. List those people skills you feel you need to improve upon.

# 2

# PEOPLE SKILLS

## Foundation of Effective Teaching

> The best teachers teach from the heart, not from the book.
>
> —Author unknown

Teaching is partly knowledge based. Academic training is where the road to becoming a teacher begins. Most complete academic training successfully.

What happens next on the road relies heavily on interpersonal or people skills. Academic training focuses on quantity of preparation with the goal of becoming a competent teacher. People skills focus on the quality of teaching. It is how you present your academic competency in the classroom.

It cannot be assumed there is a correlation between a high grade point average in college and success in teaching. Teaching is about more than grade point averages, courses taken, or degrees attained. In practice, teaching could be looked at as being based about 50 percent on knowledge and 50 percent on interpersonal skills. Is there even a possibility that teaching could be more than 50 percent based on interpersonal skills? It's something worth thinking about!

Consider the following scenario:

I worked with many teachers during my nearly thirty years as a school principal and another ten years in the area of professional development. I worked with teachers who were academically talented in their subject matter content area. These same teachers wrote exceptional lesson plans on a regular basis. However, more than a few had a very difficult time implementing their lesson plans or using their expertise in subject matter—the reason being their inadequate people or interpersonal skills. The result was less-than-effective instruction in the classroom.

On the other hand, I worked with many teachers who both possessed and demonstrated exceptional interpersonal skills in the classroom. Within this group were many who lacked expertise in their subject matter content. Their skills in writing lesson plans needed improvement. These deficiencies also led to less-than-effective instruction in the classroom.

Working with teachers in both groups, more often than not, produced similar results. Coaching, supporting, and mentoring teachers needing improvement in their content area proved successful in greater numbers than providing the same assistance to teachers struggling with inadequate classroom management—or interpersonal—skills.

Think about the implication here, even if the percentages are not completely accurate. If teaching is about 50 percent knowledge based, then completing academic training can only provide half of what it takes to become effective in the classroom. An argument could be made about the accuracy of these percentages. It depends on what research is read. However, one thing cannot be argued, and that is the need for appropriate people skills in the classroom.

Many begin teaching having successfully completed the necessary academic training resulting in a degree. Later, certain teachers come to realize that their lack of success in the classroom is related to their interpersonal skills. Their focus must then be on improving these skills.

The road to effective teaching involves both academic and people skills. The purpose of this chapter is to identify people skills needed to become an effective teacher. Although this list is not complete, it is meant to be a starting point. If the reader takes these people skills from print to practice, the results can be positive if appropriate effort is used.

★★★

Following is a list of people skills associated with effective teaching. The reader should reflect on the significance of each skill presented.

Strategy: Determine, through self-assessment, people skills you possess and those needing improvement.

Directions: In the space provided, following each people skill presented, indicate your score using the following Evaluation Scale:

1–3 means "Needs Improvement"
4–6 means "Somewhat Effective"
7–8 means "Effective"
9–10 means "Very Effective"

## 1. LIKE KIDS AND SHOW IT

Surprised with this being the first people skill mentioned toward becoming an effective teacher? Don't be! It cannot be assumed that every teacher likes kids. It *should* be assumed but reality does not prove that to be the case. Unfortunately, there are teachers who do not like kids, and many show it. Kids pick up on this attitude—some quicker than others, but eventually most get it.

This particular skill does not require teachers to go to extremes while demonstrating they like kids. However, what this skill does require is that teachers be honest in showing they care. If a teacher does not like kids, all the other people skills take on much less importance. The first people skill for the reader to take from print to practice is a most important one—but not often discussed. *Like kids and show it!* Doing so will, among other things, create a relationship of trust between teacher and students. It also establishes the foundation for effective classroom management.

Using a scale of 1 (Needs Improvement) to 10 (Very Effective), determine your score: ____

## 2. BE A GOOD LISTENER

Many teachers assume they possess good listening skills. However, in reality this could be an inaccurate assumption. Listening is a necessary skill that all teachers must have to be effective in the classroom. Improving your listening skills can improve your teaching skills.

Teaching involves all three components of communication: speaking, writing, and listening.

At some point, teachers have taken courses in speech and in writing. However, training focused on the development of listening skills is not as common. Becoming a good listener is more difficult than most people imagine. Listening is an acquired skill. Teachers must have good listening skills in addition to being academically proficient. Realize that effective communication involves more than speaking.

The following is an experience I had during my time as an elementary principal:

> As a group of primary students were leaving the lunchroom on their way to outside recess, several made comments as they passed by me. My usual response, until that day, was to say, "That's nice!" thinking that was appropriate under the circumstances. A few minutes later one of the

students returned and asked me, and I quote: "Why didn't you like my grandpa?" I told the child I didn't know his grandpa. He then asked why I said "That's nice" when he told me his grandpa just died.

Needless to say, that was a defining moment in learning to listen more effectively!

Improving listening skills requires teachers to examine their own situation in the classroom. For example, do you allow opportunities for students to participate during teaching time? Do you encourage students as they attempt to improve their verbal skills? Are classroom discussions common in your classroom? Would you describe your classroom as being teacher-centered or student-centered?

Students become active learners when teachers encourage their participation on a regular basis.

Are you a good listener or do you spend too much class time devoted to "teacher talk"? If you are not certain, try videotaping one of your lessons. View the videotape with another person you trust to be constructively critical of your performance. This would be a worthwhile activity for all teachers to try. *Be a good listener!*

Using a scale of 1 (Needs Improvement) to 10 (Very Effective), determine your score: \_\_\_\_

## 3. BE PATIENT

Interpersonal skills become extremely important when interacting with other individuals—one at a time or in groups.

Teachers interact with others every day at school. It is an ongoing activity that is repeated day after day. Interacting with students often calls for patience. Certain interactions call upon a lesser degree of patience, while others call upon a higher degree. Having patience can be the key to survival in many classroom situations.

One of the teacher's most important assets is patience. Effective teachers must be patient with their students at all times. Never lose your cool! You cannot take back behavior that has already occurred! Being a patient teacher does not in any way suggest weakness. Patience is rooted in one's inner strength and wisdom. As we all know, patience has been called a virtue. The other option, impatience, will never lead one to becoming a successful teacher. *Be patient!*

Using a scale of 1 (Needs Improvement) to 10 (Very Effective), determine your score: \_\_\_\_

## 4. HAVE A SENSE OF HUMOR

To be successful in the classroom, it is absolutely necessary to have a sense of humor. Having it and showing it are equally important. The expression "Laughter is good for the soul" takes on special meaning for teachers as they go about their work in the classroom every day.

If used appropriately, humor can become a powerful teaching tool. This is not to suggest that teachers should not be serious in situations that call for it. But having a sense of humor shows students a positive side of the teacher's personality.

However, it is important to keep in mind there is a line that exists between humor and disrespect. An effective teacher knows where that line is and should never cross it. The question is knowing how and when to use your sense of humor. Not to worry! Knowing when to use your sense of humor is instantaneous and often an involuntary reaction.

Humor is not a planned activity. You cannot insert it into your lesson plans. Obviously, some of us have a greater sense of humor than others, and that is understandable. Learning how to see humor in a given situation is a starting point for developing your own sense of humor. Learning how and when to use it is another step in the right direction. Knowing it is acceptable to laugh in the classroom is a key ingredient to having a sense of humor. It can be fun for you and your students.

Using a scale of 1 (Needs Improvement) to 10 (Very Effective), determine your score: ____

## 5. USE COMMON SENSE

Having common sense is another necessary skill in the classroom. Having common sense means being practical. It's knowing the right thing or the most appropriate thing to do in a given situation. It means recognizing what might or might not work in the classroom. Thinking before acting is an important part of using common sense.

This becomes especially important when teachers have to deal with a wide range of situations in the classroom every day. Having common sense is a huge asset toward being effective in the classroom.

Using a scale of 1 (Needs Improvement) to 10 (Very Effective), determine your score: ____

## 6. BE FLEXIBLE

The foundation for developing a successful classroom management plan depends on flexibility. It is essential that teachers be flexible in dealing with both instruction and managing student behavior. There is a close relationship between being flexible and using common sense. If one is not flexible, the assumption is that one is rigid. Being flexible gives teachers additional options in managing their classroom. Being rigid drastically reduces options available in the same situation.

Each day in the classroom is different than the day before. Everything and everyone around us is in a continuous state of change. Disruptions and interruptions are part of each day. Being flexible can minimize the impact of these occurrences. Teachers can use flexibility as a lesson in learning. As teachers model flexible behavior, it shows students how to take control of their life when they are faced with various choices.

Using a scale of 1 (Needs Improvement) to 10 (Very Effective), determine your score: ____

## 7. BE PREDICTABLE AND CONSISTENT

In the classroom, effective teachers control the environment. "Effective teachers manage their classrooms, ineffective teachers discipline their classrooms." (from Harry Wong and Rosemary T. Wong)

Effective teaching is based upon many variables. Academic competency and appropriate people skills are the two most important. Being predictable and being consistent are people skills necessary to becoming an effective teacher.

Having daily routines in the classroom allows students to know what to expect. It creates a sense of security. The predictable behavior of the teacher can promote a certain comfort level in the classroom. Being predictable also means the teacher is consistent. There are no "levels" of consistency. One is either consistent or inconsistent. For example, "No" means "No"! There is no room for negotiation when teachers are consistent in their behavior.

With appropriate effort, both predictable and consistent behavior can be improved upon when the situation calls for it.

Using a scale of 1 (Needs Improvement) to 10 (Very Effective), determine your score: ____

## 8. HAVE CONFIDENCE IN YOURSELF AND LET IT SHOW

Always remember that teaching is a very important profession. Being educated means having been taught—being taught means having worked with teachers. Teachers play an important part in all our lives.

Teaching provides a service. That service is educating students entrusted to their care. In reality, teachers assume the role and responsibility as the "daytime parent"—which is also referred to as being *in loco parentis*, translated to mean "in place of the parent." Teaching is very complex, comprehensive, and often difficult in terms of the many roles and responsibilities involved.

However, understanding the issues involved with teaching, you decided to move forward and take on whatever comes your way! You are a teacher or well on your way to becoming one. You have confidence in yourself and your ability to be effective. Confidence is a necessary people skill. Without it, you will struggle each day.

To be an effective teacher requires self-confidence. Maintaining confidence in yourself requires an ongoing effort. Some days you might question your ability to maintain your self-confidence. That is not unusual in any profession or job. It happens! But the next day is a new day when you return to your classroom. Things often look better than the day before. The important thing is to focus on maintaining your self-confidence on a regular basis. There is always tomorrow, as yesterday becomes a memory!

The following is an anonymous publication. It presents an interesting commentary on teaching:

> Nominee for "E-Mail of the Year"
> After being interviewed by the school administration, the prospective teacher said:
> "Let me see if I've got this right. You want me to go into the classroom with all those kids, correct their disruptive behavior, observe them for signs of abuse, monitor their dress habits, censor their T-shirt messages, and instill in them the love of learning.
> "You want me to check their backpacks for weapons, wage war on drugs and sexually transmitted diseases, and raise their sense of self-esteem and personal pride.
> "You want me to teach them patriotism and good citizenship, sportsmanship and fair play, and how to register to vote, balance a checkbook, and apply for a job.

"You want me to check their heads for lice, recognize signs of antisocial behavior, and make sure they all pass their final exams.

"You also want me to provide them with an equal education regardless of their handicaps and communicate regularly with their parents in English, Spanish, and any other language, by letter, telephone, newsletter, and report card.

"You want me to do all this with a piece of chalk, a blackboard, a bulletin board, a few books, a big smile, and a starting salary that qualifies me for food stamps.

"You want me to do all this and then you tell me . . . *I can't pray?*"

Using a scale of 1 (Needs Improvement) to 10 (Very Effective), determine your score: \_\_\_\_

## 9. ADMIT MISTAKES YOU MAKE

Like most people, teachers make mistakes!

Although teachers are supposed to be all-knowing about their content, mistakes can and will be made. That is not to say that it is common for teachers to make mistakes as part of their everyday teaching. When mistakes occur, it is how the teacher handles it that matters. To admit to making a mistake or to being wrong is not the easiest thing to do for most people.

However, doing so in an honest way makes it easier in the long run. One approach would be for the teacher to discuss with the students the possibility of their making a mistake. The teacher tells the students that the best way to correct the mistake is to call attention to it in a positive manner. For example, if the teacher misspells a word while writing on the chalkboard, a student should call the teacher's attention to it. No big deal because the teacher has already alerted the students how to react in such situations!

The other option is to believe teachers will not make mistakes. It then becomes a game between the teacher and the students. This is not the best option. It is better to discuss the possibility of everyone making a mistake now and then, and how to correct it in a positive way.

When the teacher admits to the possibility of making a mistake, it can create a trusting relationship in the classroom. Admitting your mistakes is a people skill needed in the classroom. It works to everyone's advantage!

Using a scale of 1 (Needs Improvement) to 10 (Very Effective), determine your score: \_\_\_\_

## 10. BE APPROACHABLE

Effective teachers are there for their students. Classrooms today are more diverse than in the past. This calls for the highest level of academic skills as well as interpersonal skills. Teachers must work with inclusionary students, the cultural diversity of students, and students having a wide range of handicaps, including those who are emotionally and behaviorally challenged. These students, along with those having differences in learning abilities, must be dealt with every day. The challenge to the teacher in today's classroom is ongoing. To be an effective teacher, challenges must be met.

In addition to other people skills, the teacher must be *approachable* to all students.

Students must understand they can go to their teacher for whatever reasons they feel important. It is important the teacher let students know this situation exists. Students in today's society face the possibility of experiencing many problems. Living in poverty is one growing reality. Many students who arrive in our classrooms are dealing with this reality every day of their lives.

Students with issues in the home are on the increase. Child abuse is a reality that teachers deal with in many classrooms.

Being approachable is a necessary people skill in the classroom. For many students, their most secure time is spent in school with their teachers.

Using a scale of 1 (Needs Improvement) to 10 (Very Effective), determine your score: _____

## 11. EXPRESS YOURSELF CLEARLY

"Teacher talk" occurs regularly in classrooms throughout each school day. It is at the core of the communicative process. Effective teachers pay attention to the amount of time during instruction spent on teacher talk. They understand that quality talk, not quantity, is very important. Too much teacher talk creates a classroom too heavily focused on the teacher. It also limits the amount of participation by students.

Communication is a two-way process. It involves speaking skills and listening skills. When teachers talk, students listen. The key to meaningful communication is clarity. Teachers must focus on clarity during instruction. The possibility exists that students did not learn a particular lesson because they did not understand it. Clarity of presentation could be the problem.

Some teachers are better communicators than others. Those assigned the job of observing and/or evaluating teachers have the responsibility to inform teachers when they need to improve their communication skills.

Another problem that exists in some classrooms is the proper use of the voice. Simply stated, some teachers speak so softly that students have to make an effort in order to hear what is being said during instruction. Other teachers speak so loudly that it actually turns students off. Both these tonal issues could lead to problems in the area of classroom management. It means the teacher must either turn the volume up or down—a problem easily corrected.

Using a scale of 1 (Needs Improvement) to 10 (Very Effective), determine your score: \_\_\_\_

## 12. USE BODY LANGUAGE EFFECTIVELY

Body language refers to using movement of the body and the use of gestures as a means of nonverbal communication. In the classroom, the use of body language can never be overstated. It occurs constantly. It is an essential part of communication. Everyone participates in the use of body language. We can say a lot with body language without uttering a single word!

Using gestures can communicate feelings such as being upset or annoyed, angry or happy. The way you position your arms, use your hands, or even the way you stand makes a statement. Eyes provide an important use of body language. Facial expressions convey a multitude of communication.

The use of body language accounts for a large part of how we communicate. Used appropriately, body language can be an important asset for teachers in terms of effective communication. However, using body language and gestures inappropriately can create problems that could escalate into serious situations. Often it is not what you say, it is how you say it through the use of body language.

Using a scale of 1 (Needs Improvement) to 10 (Very Effective), determine your score: \_\_\_\_

## 13. BE EMPATHETIC

Being empathetic means the ability to put yourself in someone else's place—to see yourself as others see you.

In the classroom this refers to looking at the problem or situation from the student's point of view. Showing empathy conveys a message of caring and understanding. Looking at yourself through the eyes of someone else should create a time for self-reflection. Being empathetic is another people skill that can contribute to successful teaching.

Using a scale of 1 (Needs Improvement) to 10 (Very Effective), determine your score: _____

## 14. BE WILLING TO REVIEW AND RETEACH WHEN NECESSARY

Students sense it and teachers need to recognize it: There are times when a lesson needs to be reviewed or retaught. Some lessons are successfully learned by students; some lessons are not. Effective teachers need to recognize the differences. It should never be assumed that every lesson is effectively delivered. Teachers need to be on alert when a particular lesson needs reviewing or needs to be retaught.

A key indicator is how well most students do on the assessment of a specific lesson. If several students do poorly on whatever assessment the teacher uses, it could suggest the lesson was not well presented. An effective teacher will readily recognize the necessity to look closely at why students did poorly when assessed and fix the problem. Teacher judgment comes into play at this time.

Reviewing or reteaching a lesson is not unusual. What is unusual is when a teacher does not have the insight to determine when doing so is necessary! There will be times when only certain students, not the entire class, will need to have the lesson reviewed or retaught.

Using a scale of 1 (Needs Improvement) to 10 (Very Effective), determine your score: _____

## DISCUSSION QUESTIONS

1. In your opinion, identify the five most important people skills discussed in this chapter. Write a rationale for each.
2. Identify the two people skills you feel are of least importance. Write a rationale for each.
3. Comment on the following statement: "A teacher's major responsibility is to present content. That is what they are trained to do. People skills play a much lesser role in terms of contributing to successful teaching and learning."
4. Which is easier to improve—academic skills or people skills? Write a rationale for your choice.
5. To what extent do people skills contribute to effective teaching?
6. Identify additional people skills you feel could be added to those presented.

# 3

# MANAGING TO TEACH

## Print-to-Practice Strategies

> Teaching is the profession that teaches all the other professions.
>
> —Author unknown

The definition of classroom management is "creating a classroom environment where the most effective teaching and learning can take place."

Successful teachers bring the following characteristics to their classroom:

- They are effective classroom managers.
- They demonstrate mastery of subject and content area.
- They have high expectations for all students.
- Their methods and approaches are based on their beliefs and understandings about how children learn.
- Their teaching personality facilitates student learning.

There is no specific order of importance for these characteristics; each is important in its own right, and together they define the successful teacher. (Richard T. Scarpaci, *A Case Study Approach to Classroom Management*. Boston: Pearson, 2007)

The evidence is clear. The number one concern of teachers, beginning or experienced, is the feeling of inadequacy when dealing with student behavior in their classroom. This problem has existed for decades. No magic exists that can provide this skill for teachers.

It is obvious that students are more likely to learn in an environment in which they feel comfortable. Being in a classroom that is chaotic does not contribute to a positive learning situation.

Students arrive in the classroom each day with a variety of attitudes that can range from cooperative to belligerent. Teachers need to understand that not all students feel good about being in school, and some don't want to be there at all. Student attitudes create a challenge to the teacher each day in the classroom.

The strength of the teacher's people skills comes into play at this point in terms of effectively managing student behavior. Before teaching can occur, the students must be ready to learn.

Following are five key points to keep in mind when focusing on classroom management strategies:

- An effective teacher manages by using positive discipline, whereas an ineffective teacher manages by using negative discipline in the classroom.
- The number one problem in the classroom is not the lack of discipline but the lack of procedures.
- To effectively manage a classroom, teachers must understand the types and causes of misbehavior.
- The only person you are able to control in the classroom is yourself.
- The ultimate goal of discipline is self-discipline.

Following are some strategies intended to assist teachers in managing their classroom.

## 1. HAVING A POSITIVE MIND-SET

Strategy: Focus on positive experiences that bring about good feelings about yourself—think happy thoughts. We all have them—if not, find some!

Here's the definition of *mind-set*: "The state of mental readiness the teacher brings to the classroom each day." Attitudes are at the core of one's mental readiness and mind-set. The absence of an appropriate mind-set can cause problems related to classroom management.

In practice, this means coming to class with a positive attitude. Demonstrating such an attitude day after day, week after week, class after class, is not always easy. Staying positive is as important as being positive. It's putting on a happy face! Remember, a smile is free and costs you nothing—and it is contagious!

The other choice is to display a negative attitude. Negative attitudes or mind-set can easily be noticed by students. The result could be reflected in how students respond with their attitudes and behaviors. Hence, a bad day in the classroom could occur for both students and teacher. Ask yourself if you ever experienced a time in a classroom where the negative attitude of the teacher was obvious, and how it affected the teaching/learning environment.

Every day will not be a blue-ribbon day in terms of having a positive mind-set. The strategy here is for the teacher to make every effort to keep the students from knowing. Better said: "Fake it till you make it!" This is a skill as well as a strategy, but one that will contribute to effectively managing your classroom.

## 2. PREPARING FOR THE START OF THE NEW SCHOOL YEAR

Strategy: Get ready physically and mentally! Plan to set aside as much time as you need to feel confident that all is in order to start the new year. Leave nothing to chance.

- As you prepare, keep in mind that first impressions only happen once.
- Get to know your students. Take time to become knowledgeable about them. Access all the information available at the school that will be helpful to you.
- Student records are a good source to begin this search. In addition to student academic records, look for such things as involvement in school activities and any honors or recognition received.
- Determine the most appropriate way to introduce yourself to students and parents before the first day of school. You might consider mailing a welcome note to each student. Students and parents should appreciate this gesture on your part. It is a great way to set the stage for the coming school year.
- Another way might be to make a personal phone call to the home. Introducing yourself in this way can also create a positive image of you and the school to parents and students alike. The effort may be worth the time involved.

- Many schools schedule activities for teachers, students, and parents to meet before the school year begins. This provides a face-to-face opportunity to get to know the students and their parents. Make every effort to participate!

## 3. ORGANIZING THE PHYSICAL ARRANGEMENT OF YOUR CLASSROOM

Strategy: Determine how placement of classroom furnishings can best accommodate successful teaching and learning. Create more than one alternative to achieve this goal.

- Determine the physical arrangement of furniture based on your plan for classroom management. Student proximity to each other becomes an important consideration. Keep in mind that seating arrangements of students can be changed. If this becomes necessary, have a purpose in mind. Never make it a random practice.
- Determine the best arrangement for other classroom furniture such as the teacher's desk, learning centers, technology items, and other resource materials. When arranging furniture and other items in the classroom, always keep safety and health issues as an important consideration.
- Observe what arrangements work in other classrooms.

## 4. THE FIRST DAY OF SCHOOL

Strategy: Review and rehearse your plans for the first day of school. What happens on this day is similar to laying the foundation when building a house. Every activity and behavior that follows will be built upon it.

- Welcome your students as they arrive. If possible, recognize each student individually.
- Have some type of "getting to know you" activity. Post seating charts available or have other directions planned. The nature and type of such an activity should, of course, be age- and grade-level appropriate. Introduce yourself and have students introduce themselves to the class at this time.
- Discuss expectations you have of the students, as well as allowing students to explain their expectations of you. Discuss rules or

guidelines that will be followed and consequences involved for breaking rules. Allow for student comments or questions.
- Discuss a typical day in your classroom.
- Discuss the process used for student grading.
- Review procedures for emergency drills so that students are well informed before they happen. Providing this information is an important safety issue.
- Entertain questions from the students. This activity will allow for student participation on the first day of school.
- End the class period or day with a positive statement. Never send students from your classroom with negative feelings.
- Always keep in mind that students spend the greater part of their day in school.

## 5. IDENTIFY AND LEARN THE STANDARDS YOU ARE RESPONSIBLE FOR TEACHING

Strategy: Learn the standards related to your subject matter. Determine how you will integrate them into your lesson plans.

The focus is on teaching the standards. There are state standards, school district standards, and individual school standards. Your knowledge and understanding of these standards and your responsibility to teach them is required in all schools. Standards must be identified and integrated into your daily lesson plans. Instruction must be aligned to the standards that are in place. Student academic progress will be assessed in terms of their learning the standards. Some schools require standards be posted in classrooms and be used as a source or reference for teaching. Teaching to the standards becomes a part of your appraisal during observational visits from your administrator. Teaching to the standards is a serious matter in schools today. Be focused on this responsibility at all times.

## 6. SETTING EXPECTATIONS FOR BEHAVIOR

Strategies:

- Have a well-written classroom management plan in place. How to deal with student behavior should be addressed in detail in this plan.
- Communicate behavioral expectations periodically with students.

- Be willing to enforce all classroom rules. An example of a rule would be: "Be respectful of others and their belongings."
- Always be firm, fair, and predictable when dealing with student misbehavior. Consequences must always fit the offense.
- Use discipline appropriately. The purpose of discipline is to teach self-discipline, not to be used as a means of punishment.
- Develop a toolbag of proactive responses to misbehavior. Include the following in your toolbag: nonverbal cues, eye contact, body gestures, proximity (be in all places in the classroom), and temporarily halting instruction.
- Never allow students to challenge you to the point that you either lose your cool or become combative. Either of these behaviors could cause the situation at hand to get seriously out of control.
- Be mindful not to create "teacher-caused" behavioral problems. Do not humiliate students, do not make threats that everyone knows cannot be carried out, avoid using a loud voice to talk over students. Do not embarrass students at any time.
- Make every effort to predict student misbehavior by recognizing cues and circumstances that serve as signals.
- Do not punish the class for the misbehavior of a few students.
- Make every effort to isolate the cause of the misbehavior and deal directly with it.
- Always be proactive; avoid becoming reactive.

Teachers are remembered for their academic skills as well as their interpersonal skills when working with students. Merging these two skills produces a classroom environment that can lead to positive student achievement.

## 7. VARIETY IS IMPORTANT IN ALL SITUATIONS, INCLUDING TEACHING

Strategy: Develop lesson plans that incorporate a variety of teaching methods and activities. This will increase the probability of engaging student interest, attention, and participation, as well as making teaching relevant.

As mentioned previously, teaching has some similarity to performing on a stage. However, in the classroom your audience will not always be ready or interested in listening to the presenter. Therefore, creating lesson plans with a variety of teaching presentations can increase the level of student engagement.

Capturing the attention of students is instrumental in having a teachable moment. Student participation is a key factor as you determine various teaching methods and activities.

## 8. VALUING DIVERSITY IN THE CLASSROOM

Strategy: Learn about your students' cultural backgrounds, values, and learning styles.

Today's classrooms are becoming more culturally diversified. Student mobility contributes to this situation. Understand that each culture includes differences (as well as similarities), related to beliefs, values, understandings, practices, and expectations.

These differences and similarities play a significant role in how students perceive and process learning experiences. These differences could relate to reading level, athletic ability, interpersonal skills, and religious beliefs—and the list goes on.

As the teacher, you must recognize the cultural differences and experiences of your students. Become knowledgeable about the beliefs and history of these cultures. Understanding the cultural diversity of your students can assist you in creating meaningful lesson plans. It will provide a great learning experience for you and your students.

Teaching in a diverse classroom can be both challenging and rewarding. Make it work for you!

Learning about cultural diversity does not just happen. Pursuing experiences such as professional development workshops and observing other culturally diversified classrooms can prove to be beneficial. Having discussions with other teachers can also be worthwhile. The importance of being a lifelong learner applies here.

## 9. MAKE YOUR CLASSROOM INVITING

Strategy: Create an attractive environment in your classroom. Make it a place where students feel comfortable and welcome.

Keep in mind that students spend most of their waking hours in school. The appearance of your classroom can contribute to motivating students to learn. Recall some of the classrooms where you spent many hours. Do you remember any particular classrooms where you felt more comfortable than others?

Elementary teachers traditionally make an effort to decorate their classrooms. Such an effort tends to be less noticeable in secondary classrooms. This should not be the case. Older students appreciate an inviting environment as much as younger students do!

### 10. "CAUGHT BEING GOOD"

Strategy: Implement a program for recognizing appropriate student behaviors as they happen. These behaviors should demonstrate extra effort made by the student.

It is a common practice for teachers to develop rules and consequences for misbehavior in their classrooms. Developing a program that is focused on catching students in an act of good behavior is not a common practice. Students expect rules in their classroom and know they are necessary. However, students do not expect to find a program for catching them in an act of good behavior, or making that extra effort.

Implementing such a program can lead to creating effective student-teacher relationships. Such a program could also contribute to improving classroom management skills of the teacher. It definitely sends a message to students that the teacher cares. It also supports a positive climate in the classroom.

### 11. USE APPROPRIATE CONSEQUENCES FOR MISBEHAVIOR

Strategy: The use of consequences in the classroom is twofold in nature. One relates to responding to positive behavior of students. The second relates to responding to negative behavior of students. Discuss both types of consequences with students. Repeat the discussion when necessary.

Using the word *consequences* in the classroom often brings negative thoughts to mind. It is necessary to understand the importance of using positive consequences recognizing appropriate student behavior. Doing so creates good feelings within the student.

Receiving grades as a result of good work is an example of a positive consequence. Hard work produces a positive result, or consequence! Students who become actively engaged in a particular lesson should be verbally praised by the teacher as a positive consequence. Students working cooperatively with the teacher and their classmates during learning activities provides an opportunity for recognition by the teacher as a positive consequence for such behavior.

As the manager of the classroom, the teacher must work hard at minimizing misbehavior. Recognizing the signs of misbehavior before it occurs is important, as it can lessen or even eliminate the problem.

Too-frequent use of punishment as a negative consequence should be avoided as often as possible. The goal should be to encourage students toward becoming self-disciplined. Of course, this may be easier said than done! However, it must remain as a goal of the teacher in trying to improve negative behavior and hopefully minimize the use of punishment.

Classrooms at all grade levels need rules or guidelines. When groups of people are assembled in one location, it becomes not only necessary but understandable that certain rules must be in place. A classroom of students is an example of such an assembled group.

Classroom rules should be the result of collaborative thinking of both students and teacher. Classroom rules should be stated positively. Safety should always be considered when developing classroom rules or guidelines. No rule should be developed unless the teacher is willing to enforce it. Violating established classroom rules is often the cause and source of student misbehavior.

When dealing with consequences to behavior, whether positive or negative, always be consistent.

There are additional strategies that can assist teachers in effectively managing their classroom. Those presented in this chapter are meant to be a starting point. Each of these strategies can be taken from print to practice with appropriate effort by the teacher. Some will require more time to implement than others, due to the nature of the strategy.

Classrooms have changed dramatically over the past several years. These changes affect classroom management skills. These changes have intensified the need for appropriate and relevant teaching strategies as well.

1. Diversity
    - Increase in number of non-English-speaking students
    - Increase in number of students from different cultures
    - Increase in number of students with disabilities
2. Children living in poverty
3. Inclusion vs. mainstreaming

4. Differing parenting styles
   - Traditional families
   - Nontraditional families
   - Single parents
   - Caregivers
5. Student mobility.

Managing to teach has moved far beyond the presentation of content material. The role and responsibilities of the classroom teacher continue to become more complex and demanding. Society has placed a wide range of expectations on today's teachers.

## DISCUSSION QUESTIONS

1. Interpret the significance of the motto: "Winning students over—not winning over them."
2. Identify strategies that might be useful for creating a healthy mind-set.
3. React to the following statement: "Dealing with student misbehavior is a major concern of classroom teachers."
4. Define "teaching in a diverse classroom."
5. Identify the pros and cons involved when using a "Caught Being Good" program in your classroom.
6. State three rules you feel are necessary in a classroom. Write a rationale for each choice.
7. Students spend many of their waking hours in the classroom. Identify three things a teacher can do to create an environment that says "Welcome."
8. Rules and standards for behavior have been set for your classroom. After unpleasant classroom experiences have occurred, students made the following comments to you. How would you respond to each of the following:
   - "I am going to tell the principal what a bad teacher you are!"
   - "Who needs to learn this stupid stuff anyway?"
   - "I can't learn anything the way you teach!"
   - "You're not fair. No other teacher gives us weekend homework!"
   - "It's your fault I failed this test. You didn't give enough time to get ready."

# 4

# THE CLASSROOM MANAGEMENT PLAN

## Bringing It All Together

> Good teaching is one-fourth preparation and three-fourths theater.
>
> —Gail Godwin

The classroom management plan provides definition for the learning environment. It sets the tone for the relationship among teachers, students, and parents. It becomes the blueprint for the instructional program.

Many teachers will admit there is no such thing as being overprepared when it comes to teaching. Without adequate preparation, confusion and chaos can occur in the classroom. Lack of preparation is a weakness and reflects on the effectiveness of the teacher. Successful teachers are prepared.

Creating a classroom management plan is a prerequisite for a successful school year. It is a road map that needs to be in place before the journey begins and students arrive for the new school year.

Two overall considerations to keep in mind when writing a classroom management plan are the following:

1. Focusing on an effective instructional program
2. Creating a classroom environment that will be welcoming and promote student engagement

These are other important issues to consider when writing your classroom management plan:

- Being fair and consistent
- Creating a positive learning environment
- Using praise and encouragement

- Providing interesting, challenging, and differentiated learning activities
- Being clear about expectations relating to both instruction and classroom behavior
- Keeping students busy and allowing no time to be wasted
- Providing a caring and safe environment
- Respecting every student
- Establishing classroom rules and consequences (with student input)
- Aligning your management plan with schoolwide policies and procedures

Children are expected to come to school ready to learn. Teachers are expected to be ready to teach. Parents send their children to school to receive a quality education. They expect the school environment to be safe, orderly, and well supervised.

A classroom management plan is only a plan. Plans can change, be amended, revised, or rewritten. A classroom management plan reflects the teacher's philosophy, personality, style, and beliefs and therefore is individualized by nature. No one plan fits all!

Having an effective classroom management plan in place sets the stage for a positive classroom learning environment.

The classroom management plan brings it all together. It includes teaching strategies and the people skills needed for those strategies to be instructionally effective. Writing a good classroom management plan requires thoughtful preparation. It needs to include both short- and long-term goals for the school year.

Use the following guidelines when writing a classroom management plan:

1. It must include age- and grade-level-appropriate instructional practices.
2. It must provide for the cultural diversity of students.
3. It must be written with clarity—a major objective.
4. It should be flexible and allow the possibility of being amended or restructured. No two classes are the same.
5. It should identify both student and teacher expectations.
6. It should include grading and assessment procedures.
7. It should address the role of the parent in the instructional program.
8. It should include behavioral expectations and related consequences for violating them.

Classroom management plans reflect the philosophy, beliefs, and style of the teacher. No two classroom management plans will be identical in content or goals—the reason being that each plan is to be used only by the teacher who created it.

Following are five models of classroom management plans. No two are exactly alike. They do, however, share some similar features. The purpose of presenting these models is to give the reader the opportunity to review their content. They are also intended to provide the reader reason to reflect on what constitutes a classroom management plan that might work effectively for them.

## MODEL 1

### Philosophy

My classroom management philosophy will be student centered and focused on providing an effective instructional program that includes all students. My instructional program will be collaborative and continually address the needs of all students. My classroom will provide a safe and orderly environment at all times.

### Classroom Environment

Daily instruction will focus on participation of students in the learning process. Students will have the opportunity to work in groups as well as on individualized learning activities. The physical arrangement of the classroom will adapt to the nature of the lesson being presented. Furniture arrangements will provide for various types of learning activities, including group projects and presentations. In determining the arrangement, consideration will be given to making furniture, supplies, and technology readily available for student use.

### Parent Involvement

My goal is to develop a program to involve parents in the instructional program of their students.

This program will be implemented during the first days of each school year. A parent welcome letter will be sent home with each student. It will include the learning objectives for students and class rules. Parents will be asked to acknowledge receipt of this initial communication.

Phone calls to parents will be made as needed, with the purpose of communicating the progress of their child in my classroom. The goal of this type of parent contact will be positive and collaborative in nature. A second goal will be to create dialogue with parents.

*Management Procedures*

My focus will be on teacher/student teamwork in creating a plan that identifies classroom rules and consequences for breaking the rules. Student self-discipline and accountability for their own behavior must be the desired outcome of any plan as it relates to effective classroom management.

*Classroom Safety*

My classroom will be an environment in which caring, wellness, student engagement, and trust exists on a daily basis. Everyone must be made aware of the need for and importance of maintaining both physical and emotional stability in the classroom at all times. An emergency plan must be in place, understood, and practiced in case of a classroom or school emergency.

*Assessment*

Procedures for grading and evaluation will be communicated to students and parents on a regular basis starting early in the school year. These procedures will include paper assessments, as well as student and parent conferences. Samples of student work will be sent home regularly for parent review and comments. I will be available to parents to discuss their child's progress at mutually agreeable times.

## MODEL 2

*Philosophy*

I believe:

- All children can learn, given appropriate time and effort.
- Students learn in different ways, at different times, and for different reasons.
- Students are motivated by being engaged, successful, and encouraged.
- My classroom management plan must align with the policies of the school.
- Students learn best when they enjoy their learning activities.
- My teaching style will be authoritative, not authoritarian or permissive.

*Principles and Core Values*

- Be fair in all circumstances.
- Criticize the behavior, not the student.
- Be assertive without being aggressive.
- Apologize when I am wrong.
- Admit mistakes I might make.
- Treat all students as individuals.
- Maintain a positive mind-set.
- Make learning engaging and challenging.
- Model the behavior I expect from students.

*Behavioral Management*

- Engage students in meaningful learning activities.
- Be proactive rather than reactive.
- Inspire others.
- Take advantage of opportunities to grow professionally. Be a lifelong learner.
- Define and model good behavior at all times.
- Teach self-discipline, not punishment.
- Show a sense of humor.
- Make use of appropriate body language.

*Routines*

- Greet students at the door as they arrive in my classroom.
- Start each class with age-appropriate opening activities.
- Use a seating chart when necessary.
- Command silence when I am speaking.
- Review the lesson objectives at the end of each class.
- End each class with an orderly exit.

# MODEL 3

*Classroom Procedures*

- Start class with minimal distractions.
- Promote critical thinking skills during instruction.
- Provide students with feedback related to their academic performance.

- Maintain an attractive learning environment in the classroom.
- Have clear objectives for instruction.
- Provide necessary classroom resources for student use, including technology.

*Communication*

- Require students to communicate in a respectful manner at all times.
- Inappropriate language is never permitted.
- Develop the use of effective listening skills for students and teacher.
- Recognize the importance of each student's contribution during instruction.

*Behavioral Management*

- Promote self-discipline not punishment.
- Recognize the dignity of each student.
- Teach the connection between behavior and consequences, both positive and negative in nature.
- Be consistent at all times.
- Involve students when developing classroom rules and consequences.

*Grading Procedures*

- Review regularly with students.
- Discuss grading procedures with students and parents.
- Align grading procedures with those of the school.
- Do not allow misbehavior to affect student grades. Keep the two separate.
- Allow students to question grades they receive.
- Provide students with additional help, if necessary or requested.

*Parent Involvement*

- Develop a system of communication that includes teacher expectations related to their child's instructional program.
- Be approachable when working with parents.
- Provide opportunities for parents to be involved in their child's program at school.

- Respond to all inquiries from parents within an acceptable time frame.

## MODEL 4

*Purpose*

A classroom management plan describes student behavior in the school environment, the classroom being the focus. A successful plan identifies rules and consequences. It also identifies standards of behavior that should be easily understood by students.

1. Develop clearly written rules. The number of rules should be determined by students working collaboratively with the teacher.
2. Rules should be written using positive language. Avoid negative words or phrases.
3. Determine consequences when rules are violated. Consider age and ability of students.
4. Reward positive behavior.
5. Communicate classroom rules and consequences with parents. Provide a handout for students to take home and review with their parents.
6. Post rules in the classroom so that students are aware of them during the entire school year.
7. Be flexible. If necessary, amend or revise rules.

## MODEL 5

This model provides an outline of content for writing a classroom management plan. This model allows the teacher the opportunity to individualize the preparation of the plan.

Part 1: Introduction
Part 2: Expectations of the Teacher
Part 3: Expectations of the Student
Part 4: Rules and Consequences
Part 5: Classroom Procedures
Part 6: Parent Involvement
Part 7: Grading and Assessment

## DISCUSSION QUESTIONS

1. Identify the difference between classroom management plans and lesson plans.
2. Why is it necessary to have a classroom management plan in place?
3. Discuss how student self-discipline can be taught and/or modeled.
4. Define the term *cultural diversity*.
5. How do teachers provide for cultural diversity when preparing classroom management plans?

# 5

# THE HOME-SCHOOL CONNECTION

## CLOSING THE GAP BETWEEN THE PARENTS AND THE SCHOOL

Engage parents in partnerships based on respect and shared interests.
Initiate contact before problems arise.
Design a variety of activities throughout the school year for parents.
Hire staff who demonstrate effectiveness when working with parents.

Many are familiar with the saying "It takes a village to raise a child." No implication for this phrase is greater than its relevance to educating a child. In this situation, the village includes the home-school connection. When schools and families work together, children tend to perform better in school, stay in school longer, and like school better.

A report published in 2004 by the Southwest Educational Development Laboratory (SEDL, Metairie, LA) was based on a decade of research related to parent involvement in schools. This report found that regardless of family background or income, students with involved parents are more likely to

- Earn higher grades and test scores
- Attend school regularly
- Pass their classes and be promoted
- Have better social skills
- Demonstrate acceptable behavior
- Adapt better to change
- Graduate
- Continue their education after high school

Many parents remember the first day they sent their child off to school with a dream about their child's future. However, evidence exists that many parents ignore the importance of regular communication with their child's school. Parent involvement is one of the most important influences on student success in school. A good relationship among the teacher, parent, and student allows all three parties to have a common understanding of learning goals.

Everyone benefits when parent and family involvement occurs in the educational setting. Most parents want to know what is going on in their child's school. Principals want to keep teachers and parents as satisfied as possible. Teachers understand that having parents on their side improves student behavior and achievement. At every level from preschool to high school, parent involvement enhances education for students, parents, and teachers.

There are parents facing major problems in their lives such as unemployment, homelessness, or lack of support from others. Dealing with and trying to solve their own problems sometimes prevents these parents from being able to meet the educational needs of their children.

There are other reasons why parents are not involved in their child's education. Some reasons are simple, some more complex. There are parents who do not have transportation and find it difficult getting from home to the school. Some parents have child-care issues, young children in the home who cannot be left alone. Sometimes employers of working parents will not allow them time off without cutting their pay. Due to the increase of diversity among our parent population, language barriers could make meeting with their child's teacher an uncomfortable experience.

A major responsibility of every teacher is to inform parents about their child's progress in school. Parents and teachers hopefully share the same goals when it comes to their child's education.

Keeping all parents informed, as well as providing opportunities for their involvement, could include the following:

1. Weekly folders. Communicate with parents in writing by sending home graded classwork. Include appropriate comments on behavior as well as other necessary information.
2. Telephone calls. Start the school year by establishing dialogue with parents. Inform parents of something positive about their child. This could include mentioning a good grade or some other type of good news. Make this initial telephone contact with parents a mutually satisfying experience. This will make the parents feel comfortable

about receiving future telephone calls, even though the message will not always be totally positive.
3. Plan conference times and dates together. Schedule time for parent conferences in late afternoon, making it more convenient for parents who work to attend. Another option would be to plan a conference before the start of the school day. If neither of these options seems convenient for parents, schedule a time for a telephone conference. The important issue is to maintain regular communication with parents, with the goal of keeping them updated on their child's in-school experiences.
4. Parent surveys. Sometime during the first few weeks of the new school year, develop a survey aimed at gathering information about the child and the home. Use the results of the survey during your first parent conference. The survey provides a starting point for the home-school connection to be successful.
5. E-mails. Today's technology provides teachers with this method of communicating with parents. It establishes an immediate two-way opportunity for communication not available in the past. Take advantage of it!

These are only a few suggestions teachers can use in establishing a meaningful home-school connection. Obviously, any attempt made toward establishing parental involvement must consider the student's age and grade level. Parents of all students, from preschool to the senior high school level, need to be involved in their child's education. No child should be left behind!

In order to educate the whole child, certain things need to happen. Effective parent-teacher communication involves asking mutually important questions. Parents want to know how their child is doing in school. Teachers need to know how the child is doing at home, especially in matters relating to their performance at school.

Interaction between teacher and parent will be helpful in the overall achievement of the child—in and out of school. It would be unusual, if not difficult, for a parent to find a school that did not welcome their involvement.

There are many ways parents can become involved at their child's school. School personnel realize that many parents have jobs and cannot physically be involved during the hours of the school day. Schools, therefore, have the responsibility of providing parents opportunities to become involved that do not require regular visits to the school during that time frame. The important consideration is that school and home work together toward identifying possibilities for parent involvement in their child's education.

Building a positive relationship with parents is essential for having a successful and rewarding school year. The goal is to establish a positive home-school connection. In too many situations, parents only become involved when they discover, one way or another, that their child is not doing well academically or behaviorally. This dilemma can be avoided in many instances with appropriate insight and proactive behavior by the school.

Building an effective home-school connection is a critical task! However, as with any relationship, mutual respect and regular communication have to occur. There has to be a continuing effort from both the school and the home.

Families whose children are doing well in school demonstrate the following characteristics:

- Establish a daily family routine related to home-school responsibilities.
- Monitor out-of-school activities.
- Model the value of learning, self-discipline, and hard work.
- Express high but realistic expectations for achievement.
- Encourage the child's progress in school.
- Encourage reading, writing, and discussions among family members.

(*What Research Says about Parent Involvement in Their Children's Education*, Michigan Department of Education Publication, 2004)

Developing parent involvement must be individualized to fit the needs of the parent and teacher involved. There are some techniques that can work in many schools. The following are some examples to consider.

## ACTIVITIES

Parents should be encouraged to support their children's education through home-learning activities. These activities might include providing for their child's wellness and proper environmental conditions that are conducive to learning. Parents can also supervise their children's homework on a regular basis. Schools should play an important role in teaching parents about their expectations for student learning.

## COMMUNICATION

Communication between home and school creates the foundation for a solid partnership. When parents and teachers communicate successfully, positive relationships develop, problems are solved more easily, and students make better progress.

Effective home-school communication is demonstrated by a two-way sharing of information important to student achievement. This communication must be regular and meaningful. Sharing must come from both parents and schools.

Schools can establish programs, such as the following, to encourage communication and strong parental involvement at the schoolwide level:

- School publications containing input from students, teachers, and parents
- Parent workshops having relevant topics
- School policies that include parent input
- Adult education programs
- Technology training programs

There is no "one-size-fits-all" for encouraging parental involvement. Therefore, each school must plan individually to meet the needs of its particular parent community.

## COLLABORATION

Schools should focus on linking parents to needed services and community organizations. Schools need to be aware of the diverse needs of their parent community.

Schools can create dialogue with local businesses, cultural organizations, and other community groups focusing on the needs of students. (J. Barrera, *An Investigation into Parent Involvement Strategies in Public Schools*. Huntsville, TX: Sam Houston State University, 2002)

In summary, the importance and need for the home-school connection cannot be overstated. Research supports this need. Achievement in school involves a triangular effort including that of the student, the school, and the parent. When any part of this triangular effort is weakened, student achievement is at risk. Children are parents' most important focus; students are the school's most important focus! When the home-school connection works effectively, the odds are in favor of everyone winning!

## DISCUSSION QUESTIONS

1. What should motivate a teacher when there is a lack of appropriate parental support?
2. Do you feel students can meet their potential in the classroom without adequate support from their parents? State a rationale for your answer.
3. The traditional home environment is changing. How can the teacher adapt to and work with nontraditional home environments?
4. Is it the responsibility of the teacher to go the extra mile when parental support is lacking in their classroom? If yes, how and why?
5. When referring to a lack of effort on the part of a particular student in her class, Mrs. Smith made the following comment: "What do you expect? The apple never falls far from the tree!" React to this statement, which obviously has parental implications.

# 6

# USING SURVEYS

> Good teachers are costly—but bad teachers cost more.
>
> —Bob Talbert

Surveys are conducted to elicit opinions from participants. The responses create data. The knowledge base held by those completing the survey has a direct impact on the degree of reliability of the results. Surveys can be designed to generate opinions or facts, depending on the nature of the survey itself.

Some surveys are scientifically constructed and are often distributed to a designated audience. Others are the product of a group or organization having a specific purpose or goal in mind when developing the survey.

Surveys presented in this chapter have a common purpose, which is to identify traits or characteristics of effective teachers and effective teaching.

The most important variable in education is the teacher. The teacher's impact on student achievement is far greater than any other influence in the school environment.

In many situations, students spend more time with their teachers than with their families. That is why it is important to continue research investigating what makes a teacher successful in the classroom. Teacher quality is an important factor in determining school quality. In simple terms, "As goes the teacher, so goes the school!"

What traits or characteristics determine teacher quality? How do you know when a teacher is effective? What evidence is needed? The answers to these questions have been the focus of educational research and surveys for many years.

One approach to finding answers is by the use of surveys. Survey respondents have identified what they feel are important characteristics of effective teachers in one survey after another.

Questions related to teacher effectiveness, and answers to them, should be of great interest to all educators.

For administrators: They have the important job of recommending and hiring teachers for employment. Their responsibility is to assign a qualified teacher in every classroom. Successful administrators understand that one of their greatest responsibilities is to provide the best education for all students. To reach this goal, administrators must provide the most qualified staff.

Robert E. Glenn published a list of fifteen traits that principals feel are most critical when employing teachers. ("Character(istics) Count! What Principals Look for When Hiring New Teachers." http://www.educationworld.com/a_admin/admin/admin257.shtml) This list is the result of a survey completed by a group of elementary and secondary principals:

- Flexibility
- Organization
- Ability to build success into the class
- Ability to communicate clearly
- Ability to create a pleasant atmosphere
- Ability to differentiate instruction
- Successful classroom management
- Enthusiasm
- High expectations
- Content knowledge
- Good people skills
- Ability to pace instruction
- Ability to ask effective questions
- Good attitude
- Ability to teach actively

For teachers: They should be aware of the skills necessary to be successful in the classroom. Important among these skills would be expertise in their content area, organizational skills, classroom management skills, being child centered in the classroom, and people skills.

For parents: They expect schools to provide a quality education for their children. They want their children to experience qualified and effective teachers. Parents expect all teachers, beginning or experienced, to be successful when working with their children. They also expect schools to have a safe and orderly environment at all times.

For communities: Good schools help create good neighborhoods. Parents and nonparents alike question the quality of the schools when considering purchasing or renting a home in the community.

In 1997, the National Association of Secondary School Principals surveyed a thousand students between the ages of thirteen and seventeen to determine those traits students most associated with the best and worst teachers. Their responses show the top five traits of each. It is logical to conclude that those teachers identified by students as "best" are also the most effective!

## TOP FIVE TRAITS OF THE BEST TEACHERS

1. They have a sense of humor.
2. They make the class interesting.
3. They have knowledge of their subject(s).
4. They explain things clearly.
5. They spend time helping students.

## TOP FIVE TRAITS OF THE WORST TEACHERS

1. They are dull and have boring classes.
2. They do not explain things clearly.
3. They show favoritism toward students.
4. They have a poor attitude.
5. They expect too much from students.

Teachers impact learning and development and may even make a difference in how the future turns out for their students.

Historian Richard Triana examined the autobiographies of 125 prominent Americans from the nineteenth and twentieth centuries. ("What Makes a Good Teacher," *Education Week*, March 2008) The survey found remarkable consistency in the descriptions given regarding the teachers these Americans admired most: (1) a command of subject matter, (2) a deep caring and concern for students, and (3) a distinctive style of teaching.

How does one become an effective teacher? What do effective teachers do? How does an effective teacher think? The answers to these questions are found in the work of prominent developmental psychologists including Jean Piaget, Lawrence Kohlberg, and Thomas Lickona. They grouped their findings into three categories.

1. Personal traits. Caring for students was the most common personal trait found in their research.
2. Teaching traits. Effective teachers encourage. They do so through use of positive words, actions, and facial expressions. Teachers provide students with the hope to keep striving to learn. These psychologists agreed that effective teachers ask probing questions to challenge accuracy and completeness of thinking in a way that moves students to their ultimate goal.
3. Intellectual traits. All the developmental psychologists agreed that one of the intellectual traits of effective teachers is to be a lifelong learner. They are as much street smart as they are book smart. These teachers have knowledge of their students and the school and the community in which they are teaching. They use this knowledge to uniquely approach each student and head off or solve problems in the classroom. Teachers who model high expectations for themselves tend to get the same results from their students.

In 2002, Corbett and Wilson surveyed four hundred students from urban middle and senior high schools to identify those things that they felt their schools could do to encourage students and enhance learning. (D. Corbett and B. Wilson, "What Urban Students Say about Good Teaching," *Educational Leadership* 60, no. 1, pp. 18–22)

Teachers were identified as the main factor in determining the quality of the students' educational experience. Some of the other comments about good teachers included:

- They involve students in their learning process.
- They explain content and assignments clearly.
- They are willing to help students individually.
- They vary classroom routines to keep class work interesting and engaging.
- They take time to get to know students.

This study clearly indicates that good teaching equals successful learning.

The following survey is the result of input and responses from students working on their master's degrees at the University of Cincinnati. The survey was conducted over a period of four years and several courses in the area of classroom management. Input was also provided by teachers-in-service during the same time period: 2006–2010.

The initial step was to construct the survey. Those participating at the time were asked to identify traits of effective teachers based upon their opinion and experience in education. Forty traits were identified.

The second step was to administer the survey. Those completing the survey were asked to rate each teacher trait using two criteria.

The first was to rate each trait as being of High (H), Moderate (M), or Low (L) importance.

The second was to rate each trait as an Academic Skill (A) or a People Skill (P). So each teacher trait was to have two ratings.

Third, after completing the survey, discussions were held with participants, focusing on the rationale for their responses.

Please complete the following survey using the directions provided. The responses of those previously taking this survey will be presented for your review on pages following the survey itself. Compare your responses to the responses of others who completed this survey.

## THE SURVEY

*Directions*

The following is a partial listing of traits of effective teachers. Please rate each trait using the following two indicators:
First: Rate each trait as being
- H = High Importance
- M = Moderate Importance
- L = Low Importance

Second: Rate each trait as being
- A = Academic Skill
- P = People Skill

| | | |
|---|---|---|
| 1. Knows learning levels of students | H/M/L | A/P |
| 2. Holds high standards for all students | H/M/L | A/P |
| 3. Makes students excited about learning | H/M/L | A/P |
| 4. Is honest and honorable | H/M/L | A/P |
| 5. Is energetic | H/M/L | A/P |

6. Demonstrates appropriate decision-making skills — H/M/L — A/P
7. Is a visionary — H/M/L — A/P
8. Is well organized — H/M/L — A/P
9. Is trusting and trustworthy — H/M/L — A/P
10. Is self-reflective — H/M/L — A/P
11. Is dependable — H/M/L — A/P
12. Is patient — H/M/L — A/P
13. Is supportive — H/M/L — A/P
14. Is fair — H/M/L — A/P
15. Is a good listener — H/M/L — A/P
16. Is approachable — H/M/L — A/P
17. Is able to challenge others and willing to be challenged — H/M/L — A/P
18. Is a good communicator — H/M/L — A/P
19. Likes kids and shows it — H/M/L — A/P
20. Takes on responsibilities willingly — H/M/L — A/P
21. Is collaborative and cooperative — H/M/L — A/P
22. Admits mistakes — H/M/L — A/P
23. Is entertaining — H/M/L — A/P
24. Has a sense of humor — H/M/L — A/P
25. Maintains order in the classroom — H/M/L — A/P
26. Is persistent, consistent, and predictable — H/M/L — A/P
27. Leaves nothing to chance — H/M/L — A/P
28. Is adaptable — H/M/L — A/P
29. Demonstrates expertise in teaching content — H/M/L — A/P
30. Creates positive student/teacher relationships — H/M/L — A/P
31. Has a well-written classroom management plan — H/M/L — A/P
32. Is intuitive — H/M/L — A/P
33. Presents a professional appearance — H/M/L — A/P
34. Demonstrates leadership qualities — H/M/L — A/P
35. Is team oriented — H/M/L — A/P
36. Develops a positive relationship with parents — H/M/L — A/P
37. Participates in professional development activities — H/M/L — A/P

| | | |
|---|---|---|
| 38. Is a lifelong learner | H/M/L | A/P |
| 39. Stays cool when under pressure | H/M/L | A/P |
| 40. Has a good attendance record | H/M/L | A/P |

## ANALYSIS OF SURVEY RESPONSES

Two considerations need to be kept in mind as the results of this survey are analyzed. First, it is a nonscientific survey. Second, the responses are opinions from respondents having various levels of experience and knowledge in the field of education.

Important consideration has been given in this book to the importance of people skills necessary to be an effective teacher.

Teaching is about people—namely, the students, whose educational achievement is closely aligned to the effectiveness of their teachers. Educating students in today's classroom has moved far beyond the teaching of content. That is not to lessen the importance of the teachers having expertise in their content area. What it does mean is that expectations are far more complex than just a few decades ago.

The nature and composition of today's classrooms is changing at rapid pace. Contributing to that change includes, but is not limited to, increase in cultural diversity, inclusionary practices, use of technology, increase in the number of students from nontraditional families, and increasing mobility of students.

The survey results show that twenty-nine of the forty traits listed (73 percent) were rated as people skills. Only eleven traits (27 percent) were rated as academic skills.

These statistics show that respondents consider people skills as being highly essential to being an effective teacher. The message seems clear: effective people skills are necessary for success in the classroom.

Of the forty traits listed, respondents rated thirty-one, or 77 percent, as being of high importance. Compare that statistic to that of the importance of people skills (73 percent). The conclusion would indicate that respondents are saying that people skills (73 percent) are of high importance (77 percent) in being an effective teacher.

This particular survey is lengthy in terms of the number of traits listed. However, it provides the opportunity to reflect upon those people skills that work successfully in today's classroom.

This survey creates a forum for discussion among those who study its results. Those who study the results might have differing opinions than those generated by the statistics shown.

Surveys have different purposes and goals. They are often evaluative, and that can be a good thing. It is possible that change in a positive direction might be a result of a survey. Surveys related to effective teachers and teaching often share many similar traits.

One important outcome of reading such a survey is that it provides an opportunity to reflect on one's own situation by considering those traits identified as important.

Following are the results of those formerly taking this survey. Keep in mind that all responses reflect the *consensus* of participants:

| | | | |
|---|---|---|---|
| 1. H/A | 11. H/P | 21. H/P | 31. H/A |
| 2. H/A | 12. H/P | 22. M/P | 32. M/P |
| 3. M/P | 13. H/P | 23. L/P | 33. H/P |
| 4. H/P | 14. H/P | 24. H/P | 34. H/A |
| 5. H/P | 15. H/P | 25. H/A | 35. H/P |
| 6. H/A | 16. H/P | 26. M/P | 36. H/P |
| 7. M/P | 17. H/A | 27. M/A | 37. H/A |
| 8. H/P | 18. H/P | 28. H/P | 38. M/A |
| 9. H/P | 19. H/P | 29. H/A | 39. H/P |
| 10. M/P | 20. H/P | 30. H/P | 40. H/P |

## DISCUSSION QUESTIONS

1. How can results of surveys be used?
2. Can one become effective in the classroom having inadequate people skills?
3. How important is it for a teacher to have expertise in the subject matter they teach?
4. Review the survey having forty traits of effective teachers. Add one you think is missing.
5. What is the difference between a scientific and nonscientific survey?

# 7

# MEETING THE CHALLENGE

> Teachers are expected to reach unattainable goals with inadequate tools. The miracle is that at times they accomplish this impossible task.
>
> —G. Ginott

Teaching includes simple, complex, and comprehensive responsibilities. In today's schools, teachers are expected to be all things to all people. Their role has greatly expanded. However, the focus still is on providing a quality instructional program that is designed to meet the needs of all students.

There are other teaching responsibilities that have remained unchanged over time. Most important among these responsibilities is the expectation that student achievement is never compromised. Mastery of subject matter content is still of major importance. Providing a safe and orderly classroom environment continues to be a high priority.

Successful teachers continue to work effectively with parents. Being a lifelong learner is still a goal for most educators. Good teachers have a classroom management plan in place that reflects their beliefs, style, and instructional goals. Successful teachers continue to work well with other colleagues in a team-based environment. These are some teacher responsibilities that have survived without major change.

However, new challenges face teachers in today's school. These new challenges have required teachers to learn new skills and insights related to their job and their responsibilities. These challenges include, but are not limited to, the following:

- Working with the nontraditional family
- Providing academic and behavioral needs for inclusionary students

- Learning to work effectively with increasing numbers of culturally diverse students in their classroom
- Getting and remaining updated in the use of technology
- Understanding homelessness and working with students and families in such situations
- Dealing with student mobility
- Working with increasing numbers of students living in poverty

In addition to these challenges, teachers must also deal with violence occurring in our schools. There are several types of school violence including dealing with child abuse, bullying, sexual abuse, theft, vandalism, and the existence of gangs. In an attempt to stop the various types of school violence, we must first learn about them. This includes studying the psychology of deviant behavior.

Dealing with school violence is a serious challenge for new as well as experienced teachers. While investigating acts of school violence it was discovered that there were students who had knowledge about acts of violence before they took place.

Teachers, as well as other school personnel, must make every effort to recognize the signs of impending acts of violent behavior. Being proactive instead of reactive could stop violent behavior from happening.

One article identified ten ways that teachers can prevent school violence:

1. Take responsibility both inside and outside your classroom.
2. Don't allow prejudice or stereotypes in your classroom.
3. Listen to "idle" chatter in your classroom.
4. Get involved in student antiviolence organizations in your school.
5. Educate yourself on danger signs in students:
   - Sudden lack of interest
   - Obsession with violent games
   - Depression and mood swings
   - Writing that shows despair/isolation
   - Lack of anger management skills
   - Talking about death or bringing weapons to school
   - Violence toward animals
6. Discuss violence prevention with students.
7. Encourage students to talk about violence.
8. Teach conflict resolution and anger management skills.
9. Get parents involved.
10. Take part in schoolwide initiatives.

(M. Kelly, "Secondary Education: Ten Ways Teachers Can Help Prevent School Violence." http://712educators.about.com/od/schoolviolence/tp/prevent_school_violence.htm, 2010)

Another study identified a number of common risk factors through a clinical interviewing process. These risk factors, according to the study, warrant immediate attention, even if the student is perceived as nonviolent. These risk factors do not mean a student is violent but only at risk.

- Violent drawings or writing
- Threats of violence to others
- History of past violent behavior
- A relationship breakup such as being jilted by a boyfriend or girlfriend
- Reports of being harassed or picked on by others
- Withdrawal from peer and family support
- Inappropriate use or access to firearms
- Substance abuse
- Called different or weird by peers
- Low interest in school

(K. Dwyer, D. Osher, and C. Warger, "Early Warning, Timely Response: A Guide to Safe Schools." Bethesda, MD: National Association of School Psychologists, 1988)

Students who have many of these identified high-risk factors may be experiencing significant emotional problems. These students may be at risk of becoming violent and are unlikely to function adequately without some type of counseling. School personnel should take notice and act appropriately and timely.

While examining school violence, a focus should be placed on four factors: the individual child, the home environment, the neighborhood environment, and the school environment.

### The Individual Child

A distinction is made between internalizing and externalizing types of behavior. Internalizing behaviors include withdrawal, anxiety, and depression. Internalizing behavior has been found in some cases of youth violence. Because they rarely act out, students internalizing problems are often overlooked by school personnel. (C. A. Christie, C. M. Nelson, and K. Jolivet, *Prevention of Antisocial and Violent Behavior in Youth: A Review of Literature.* Lexington, KY: University of Kentucky, 2005)

Externalizing behaviors refer to delinquent activities, aggression, and hyperactivity. Unlike internalizing behaviors, externalizing behaviors include or are directly linked to violent episodes. Just as externalizing behaviors are observed outside of school, such behaviors are also observed in schools.

### The Home Environment

The home environment is believed to contribute to school violence. There is evidence that suggests a child's exposure to gun violence, domestic violence, parental alcoholism, child abuse, and sexual abuse teaches them that criminal and violent activities are acceptable. (Constitutional Rights Foundation, "Causes of School Violence." http://www.crf-usa.org/school-violence/causes-of-school-violence.html)

### The Neighborhood Environment

Neighborhoods and communities can provide the environment for school violence. Communities having higher rates of drug use and crime can teach youth the violent type of behaviors that can be taken into schools. Teacher assault is more likely to occur in schools located in high-crime neighborhoods. Research has shown that poverty and high population densities are associated with higher rates of school violence. (G. W. Evans, "The Environment of Childhood Poverty." *American Psychologist* 59, no. 2, 2004, pp. 77–92)

### The School Environment

Recent research has linked the school environment to school violence. Teacher assaults are associated with a higher percentage of male faculty, a higher proportion of male students, and a higher proportion of students receiving free or reduced lunch costs. In general, a large male population, higher grade levels, a history of high levels of disciplinary problems in the school, high student-to-teacher ratios, and an urban location are related to violence in schools. (M. Limbos and C. Casteel, "Schools and Neighborhoods: Organizational and Environmental Factors Associated with Crime in Secondary Schools." *Journal of School Health*, 2008, pp. 539–44)

In order to respond to issues relating to such unsafe situations existing in schools, violence intervention programs have been developed and implemented. The goal of these programs is to teach students how to deal with conflict in nonviolent ways. Another goal is to create school environments that support peaceful behavior.

The U.S. Department of Education's 2001 *Annual Report on School Safety* included the following recommendations aimed toward helping schools become safe environments:

1. Provide strong administrative support for assessing and enhancing school safety.
2. Redesign the school facility to eliminate dark, secluded, and unsupervised spaces.
3. Devise a system for reporting and analyzing violent and noncriminal incidents.
4. Design an effective school discipline policy.
5. Build a partnership with local law enforcement.
6. Enlist trained school security professionals to design and maintain the school security system.
7. Train school staff, including support staff, in all aspects of violence prevention.
8. Provide all students with access to school psychologists and counselors.
9. Provide crisis response services.
10. Implement schoolwide education and training on avoiding and preventing violence and violent behavior.
11. Use alternate school settings for educating violent and weapon-carrying students.
12. Create a climate of tolerance.
13. Provide appropriate educational services to all students.
14. Reach out to communities and businesses to assist in improving the safety of students.
15. Actively involve students in making decisions about school policies and programs.
16. Prepare and distribute to the public an annual report on school crime and safety.

(Richard T. Scarpaci, *A Case Study Approach to Classroom Management.* Boston: Pearson Education, 2007)

A less sensational, but equally harmful, type of violent behavior is bullying. It is one of the most common types of school violence. Bullying occurs when a physically or socially powerful person injures, intimidates, or scares another, usually weaker person.

Bullying can also include group behavior. This happens when one group, feeling they have more power, intimidates another group by using some form of bullying.

Bullying is in no way a normal or acceptable part of childhood behavior. It is a purposeful act aimed at hurting others both physically and emotionally. Some refer to bullying as simply one person teasing another. There is a significant difference between teasing and bullying in terms of intent, actions, and outcome.

Each day many children of all ages go to school in fear of being bullied. It is a problem that not only affects children. It is a major concern for parents, teachers, and administrators as well. Bullies often pick on those they feel do not fit in because of how they look, dress, or act, their race, their religion, or their sexual orientation.

There are several types of bullying:

- Physical bullying involves physical contact between at least two people. The intent is to hurt or injure a person by using force such as punching, hitting, or kicking. One type of physical bullying is taking something that belongs to another and destroying it.
- Verbal bullying involves spreading lies or rumors about another person or persons. It is also repeating something told to one person in confidence to another.
- Cyber bullying involves sending messages using electronic resources. This would include the use of e-mails, voice mails, texting, or the use of the Internet. This particular type of bullying is increasing at an alarming rate due to the availability of technology.

Bullying is sometimes difficult to detect. It often occurs on crowded playgrounds and in places not as well supervised by school personnel such as restrooms, showers, stairs, or hallways.

Another favorite place for bullies to perform is on school buses. It is not unusual for bullying to take place as students walk to and from school. Although bullies enjoy demonstrating their perceived power, they are usually careful not to perform in places they can easily be caught.

Bullying creates a painful effect on its victims. Bullies usually repeat their behavior several times on their intended target. Thus, it can cause the victim to live in a constant state of fear and anxiety. The result of being bullied can lead to physical, emotional, and social problems.

Dealing with bullying is another challenge that must be met by the classroom teacher. An alert teacher will develop awareness of the problem and make consequences known to students. One method is the use of proximity in the classroom and any other locations where bullying might occur. Students then become aware of the mobility of the teacher, which might cause them to think carefully before misbehaving.

School administrators have responsibility for dealing with bullying at the school site—inside and outside. Proactive policies must be in place and consistently enforced. Consequences for engaging in the act of bullying must be communicated to the entire school community—students, teachers, parents, and the community at large. Bullying is a form of violence against others, and it cannot be tolerated in the school environment. Its effect on others can be serious and long-lasting.

It exists in some form in all schools. Two important strategies that can be used in the classroom are:

1. Teach self-discipline on a regular basis. Include discussing its meaning and importance to each student.
2. Teach conflict management skills. Focus on students respecting each other's rights and how to solve problems calmly and collaboratively.

Here are some of the differences between bullying and violence:

- While violence and violent crimes have tended to decrease in America, bullying has not.
- Violence is against the law, while bullying generally isn't unless it involves assault.
- Violence is seen as an unacceptable type of behavior, while more people accept bullying as a normal part of life.

Some common factors that may contribute to bullying and violence include the following:

- Severe physical punishments used in the home
- Lack of parental supervision and involvement
- Lack of understanding of positive ways to deal with problems

Here are some important school violence research findings:

- Bullying generally begins in the elementary grades, peaks in the sixth through eighth grades, and persists into high school. (North Carolina Department of Justice and Delinquency Prevention, 2002)
- Bullying was reported as more prevalent among males than females and occurred with greater frequency among middle-school-aged

youth than high-school-aged youth. For males, both physical and verbal bullying was common. For females, verbal bullying and rumors were more common. ("Bullying Behaviors among U.S. Youth," *Journal of the American Medical Association*, 2001)
- Research shows that those who bully and are bullied appear to be at greatest risk of experiencing the following: loneliness, trouble making friends, lack of success in school, and involvement in problem behaviors such as smoking and drinking. (North Carolina Department of Justice and Delinquency Prevention)

Child abuse is another form of violence. The result of child abuse makes its way into the school and classroom by way of the victim—the child. It is one of the most upsetting challenges facing teachers. Child abuse is nothing new. Meeting this challenge for the first time will be extremely unpleasant. For many years, child abuse was one of the most overlooked violent behaviors in our society, both in and out of the school environment.

Child abuse refers to those under the age of eighteen whose parent, or other legal caregiver responsible for his or her care, commits any of the following types of violent behavior:

- Inflicts or allows to be inflicted serious physical injury upon the child
- Creates or allows to be created a risk of physical injury
- Commits or allows to be committed a sexual offense against the child as defined by law

(Richard T. Scarpaci, *A Case Study in Classroom Management*. Boston: Pearson, 2007)

There are several types of child abuse. Some are easier to detect than others. Types of child abuse include:

- Physical abuse
- Physical neglect
- Sexual abuse
- Emotional abuse
- Educational neglect

Any school employee who suspects, or has knowledge of, child abuse is required by law to report such suspicions to appropriate authorities. Failing to do so makes that person guilty of a legal misdemeanor.

Once the report is made, it becomes the responsibility of the person receiving it to take the appropriate action that is required. The person reporting suspicion of child abuse is often concerned about being wrong and what can happen if that is true. The key word here is *suspicion*. Of course, there can be some unfortunate circumstances that follow the reporting of suspected child abuse. This is especially possible if it is proven there was no abuse involved. However, that should never prevent the teacher or other school personnel from doing what must be done.

It is the responsibility of the school principal to inform the faculty and staff of their legal duty when dealing with suspected child abuse. It is the responsibility of each member of the faculty and staff to act accordingly.

In certain communities, school violence is associated with the growth of gangs. Although youth gangs have existed in cities across the United States for many years, current trends regarding the presence of gangs has gotten the attention of school officials where they operate.

The possibility of the eruption of gang activity exists anywhere at any time. Gang leaders recruit members from young adults in their early to late teenage years; the average age for recruitment being seventeen. Often teens join gangs because they are bored, are lacking in purpose, or are looking for a way to belong. (A. Egley and M. Arjunan, "Highlights of the 2000 National Youth Gang Survey." Washington, DC: U.S. Department of Justice, Office of Justice Programs, Office of Juvenile Justice and Delinquency Prevention, 2002) In schools where gangs do exist, it becomes the responsibility of those in authority to respond in an appropriate and timely manner.

Teaching in today's schools can demand, under certain circumstances, greater effort than in the past. The role and responsibilities of classroom teachers continues to expand on a regular basis. Being academically prepared and teaching content is not enough for a today's teachers to be successful.

Effective interpersonal or people skills are extremely essential to the job. A major part of the teacher's job is meeting the numerous challenges they face each day in their classroom. However, it is critical that the focus continue to be on providing the best instructional program for all students.

## DISCUSSION QUESTIONS

1. Define the term *nontraditional family*.
2. Identify proactive behaviors a teacher can use to ease situations in the classroom that show signs of becoming violent.
3. How can conflict-management and anger-management skills be taught in the classroom?

4. In your opinion, what are the differences between bullying, teasing, and bothering others?
5. What are signs of gang affiliation a teacher can look for in the classroom?
6. How significant are interpersonal or people skills in terms of dealing with challenges that occur in the classroom?

# 8

# ENGAGING STUDENTS IN LEARNING

> Man's mind stretched to a new idea never goes back to its original dimensions.
>
> —Oliver Wendell Holmes

How often have you heard students say, "School is boring"? How often have parents asked their children "What did you learn in school today?" and have them respond "Nothing"? If indeed this were true, we would have many poorly educated students among us!

The issue of being bored in school has been around longer than we would like to imagine. Today students are expressing their discontent more openly than in years past. Many students feel that schoolwork is not connected to the real world. Indiana University's School of Education produced a report in 2006 titled *Voices of Students on Engagement: A Report on the 2006 High School Survey of Student Engagement*. This survey of more than eighty thousand students found 50 percent reported being bored in school every day, while 75 percent reported they were bored because the material wasn't interesting!

Saying that some students are bored in class isn't necessarily headline news. The good news is that we know what causes boredom and we know how to engage students. The last two decades have seen academic research on engagement and boredom offering numerous insights into how we can align classroom activities to battle boredom and engage students on a meaningful level. Teachers and schools that have made student engagement a priority have seen dramatic results. When students see the value in what they do and how they do it, they will come to see school as an important place that offers them meaningful growth and opportunities to discover their potential.

In a book titled *Battling Boredom: Ninety-Nine Ways to Spark Student Achievement* (Larchmont, NY: Eye on Education, 2011), author Bryan Harris identifies ways teachers can effectively battle boredom:

- Plan specific strategies, lessons, and techniques to engage a variety of learners. Teachers should incorporate specific strategies based on the needs of their students.
- Monitor the strategies being used and adjust to meet the needs of the students.
- Have backup strategies ready, because not every strategy works equally well with all students.
- Demonstrate enthusiasm about the content being learned as well as the methods used for learning and instruction. Teachers should exude a genuine belief that the learning and content are valuable and meaningful.
- Communicate the relevance of the content being studied. Students want to be engaged in learning that is relevant to their lives, interests, and future.
- Celebrate successes, both big and small. Success at a task is motivating and exciting, and it encourages students to continue their efforts.

Engaging students in their learning process is a goal of all teachers. It does not happen automatically! Surviving in the classroom involves engaging students in their own learning. In some classrooms, engaging students during instruction happens with little effort on the part of the teacher. However, this is not the case in many other classrooms. Students bring their own attitudes and behaviors to school every day. As one would imagine, these attitudes and behaviors range from cooperative to belligerent in terms of their willingness to participate in the learning process. If students are going to achieve, they must be engaged in the instruction going on in the classroom. The bottom line is that if the teacher does not create engaging learning activities, some students will find other ways to become engaged—and that could result in less-than-desirable situations!

Engaging all students in the instructional program creates a major responsibility and challenge for all classrooms teachers. It calls on both their academic skills and their people skills. How teachers use these skills will determine how effectively they engage their students in the learning process. In addition to being academically prepared and using appropriate people skills, major attention has to be given to the delivery of instruction. Effective instruction needs to include both content and appropriate teaching methods used to deliver it.

When creating their classroom management plan, teachers must keep in mind the importance of how instruction is presented as it relates to engaging the learner. Lesson plans must also be created in the same way. The end result of effective instruction is student achievement. Achievement occurs when students become engaged in their own learning. Putting this all together and making it happen involves great effort on the part of the classroom teacher.

A brain-based classroom is one in which students are actively engaged in learning. What exactly does it mean for students to be actively engaged? It certainly does not mean having students complete worksheets, answer basic questions, or take notes during instruction. Take a minute to think about the definitions of the words *actively engaged*. The word *active* means moving, working, participating, full of energy, and causing action. The word *engage* means to require use of/occupy, to attract and hold attention, and to involve. So basically, when students are actively engaged, they are participating and working in a way that is active, full of energy and motion, and they are involved and interested in what is being learned.

Wow! That is a lot to ask of our students, or is it more than a lot to ask of teachers? This type of learning requires much more work and effort on the part of the teacher. It is much easier to have students read a chapter, answer questions at the end, and complete a ready-made worksheet.

Many newer textbooks now include activities that engage students in their own learning. If the textbooks you are using include these types of activities, consider using those that are relevant when writing your lesson plans. (Emma McDonald, "Engaging Students in Learning—Tips and Ideas." http://ezinearticles.com/?Engaging-Students-in-Learning---Tips-and-Ideas&id=1002939)

How instruction is organized and presented has a direct effect on engaging students in their own learning. If students are to be engaged, the teacher must be engaged in teaching. Teachers need to provide frequent feedback to students so they can evaluate their own progress. Engaging students involves both a hands-on and minds-on approach!

## COOPERATIVE LEARNING: AN EXAMPLE OF AN INSTRUCTIONAL PRACTICE PROMOTING STUDENT ENGAGEMENT

Some classrooms are teacher-centered. Others are student-centered. Those classrooms that are student-centered create a greater opportunity for engaging students in their own learning. Cooperative learning is an example of a student-centered classroom. It is a teaching strategy in which small teams of students, with varying levels of ability, are involved in a variety of learning activities to improve their understanding of a given assignment. Each team member has the responsibility for their own learning but also for assisting other team members. The result is that students work collaboratively toward achievement of the individual student and of the team as a whole. It is an approach where the success of the group depends on the success of the individual, with everyone working together.

Five basic elements of cooperative learning include:

- Positive interdependence. Effort of each team member is required for success of the group.
- Face-to-face interaction. Orally explaining how to solve problems during group discussions.
- Individual and group accountability. Having each student teach others what he or she has learned.
- Social skills. Learning leadership, decision-making, trust-building, conflict-management, and communication skills.
- Group processing: Achieving goals, maintaining effective working relationships, discussing the actions of each team member.

The need for interdependence happens at all levels of our society. Creating a learning structure that provides students the opportunity to work effectively in a collaborative environment will contribute to students practicing interdependent behaviors.

Cooperative learning encourages engaging students in their own learning. Each student must be engaged during the team activities. Each student is recognized for his or her contribution to the group as the team works on the assignment. Each student learns the importance of working together. If properly organized and monitored by the teacher, the cooperative team experience will be one of positive growth in developing not only academic achievement but also in the area of improving social skills by learning how working together can be rewarding.

Cooperative learning is a great instructional practice for any classroom, including those that are culturally diverse. Cooperative learning provides a give-and-take between students and places them in both a teacher role and a student role. One of the best ways to internalize new knowledge and learn how to make the knowledge applicable is through cooperative learning. Cooperative learning in a culturally diverse classroom has the added benefit of teaching students about other cultures, behaviors, and beliefs. This is educationally productive, since each student has something to offer and the group as a whole benefits.

Research has shown that cooperative learning

- Promotes student learning and academic achievement
- Increases student retention
- Enhances student satisfaction with their own learning experience (engagement)
- Helps students develop skills in oral communication
- Promotes student self-esteem
- Helps promote positive race relations

(Spencer Kagan, *Cooperative Learning*. San Clemente, CA: Kagan Publishing, 1994)

Cooperative learning improves critical thinking, self-esteem, multicultural relations, and positive social behaviors more than using traditional teaching approaches. (T. Cooper, *Cooperative Learning and Instruction: Effective Use of Student Learning Teams.* Long Beach, CA: University Academic Publications Program, 1990) A 1993 study involving more than twenty-seven thousand students concluded that student-student interactions and student-faculty interactions, both basic teamwork components, are the most important influences on academic success and satisfaction. (A. Astin, *What Matters in College? Four Critical Years Revisited.* San Francisco: Jossey-Bass, 1993)

## STUDENT-CENTERED CLASSROOM: AN EXAMPLE OF ENGAGING STUDENTS IN THEIR OWN LEARNING

The traditional classroom involves teacher-directed instruction. Teacher talk consumes most of the time during instruction. Students, for the most part, are in a passive mode.

Teacher-directed instruction involves:

- Students respond to teacher expectations.
- Students are given extrinsic rewards such as grades.
- Student work is evaluated by the teacher.
- Students complete assignments created by the teacher.

The student-centered classroom involves focusing on the needs of students, not teachers. It places students first, in comparison to teacher-centered learning in the traditional classroom. Students' contributions are at the core of the learning experience. Teacher-centered classrooms have the teacher as the core learning experience and place students in a passive role. In the student-centered classroom, students are required to be active, responsible, and participate in their own learning. A variety of hands-on learning experiences are presented, with the goal of promoting successful learning.

Student-centered teaching actively engages students in their own learning experience. The following list provides a few examples of why student-centered learning is important:

- Strengthens student motivation
- Promotes peer communication
- Reduces disruptive behavior
- Builds student-teacher relationships
- Promotes discovery/active learning
- Strengthens responsibility for one's own learning (engagement)

*(Wikipedia)*

The student-centered classroom is a contrast in function and purpose to the traditional, teacher-directed classroom. In the student-centered classroom, students take a much greater role and responsibility for their own learning. They are continuously engaged in learning. They are required to take ownership for their own work. Teachers perform in the role of coach, mentor, and facilitator to their students. In the student-centered classroom, the focus on activities shifts from the teacher to the student.

Because of the openness of the student-centered classroom, learning content provides students the opportunity to discover their own learning styles. Successful learning occurs when students become fully engaged in an active learning process. The teacher's goal, as a facilitator, is to guide students into finding new interpretations of the learning material.

To implement a student-centered learning environment, attention must be given to the following aspects of learning:

- What students are curious about learning
- What teaching strategies are needed to accommodate student needs
- The social needs of students such as peer approval and communication skills

Not all teachers will feel comfortable or interested in teaching in a student-centered environment. It means relinquishing much of the control that exists in the traditional classroom. One particular issue is allowing students to participate in their own assessment rather than having the teacher assign grades. All things considered, the student-centered classroom provides a great opportunity to engage students in their own learning.

## STUDENT SELF-ASSESSMENT AS A TECHNIQUE FOR ENGAGING STUDENTS IN THE CLASSROOM

The ability to self-assess is critical to ongoing learning in the classroom. Allowing students to take an active role in evaluating their own work, instead of evaluations being the result of observations by others, helps them discover relevance for their own learning.

Self-assessment contributes to students' self-confidence. Through continued practice of self-assessment, students can learn what it means to make an informed, responsible judgment of their own and another's performance. They experience increased confidence in their own judgment when they can validate performance for themselves. (G. Loacker, *Self-Assessment*. Milwaukee, WI: Alverno College Institute, 2000) Any technique or teaching strategy that allows students to participate in their own learning creates the opportunity for engaging them in the instructional program.

The goal of effective teachers is to have their students learn and be successful. The success that students experience depends on how much they are engaged in their own learning. It is the teacher's responsibility to create learning activities that challenge students. These learning activities must require the students to think. At the same time, these learning activities must be relevant and meaningful so the students can see the purpose in what they are learning.

Engaging students in the classroom requires continuous attention. Having a good classroom management plan and well-written lesson plans contributes to this effort. But it doesn't stop there! A key concept is *connecting* with your students! Connecting is when you, as the teacher, recognize students individually and value their ideas. It means you know the skills they possess and those they need to learn. Connecting happens every day when you respond to students in your classroom as they participate and express their need for help and support. Connecting is *caring*. Teachers who care teach from the heart, not only the book!

## DISCUSSION QUESTIONS

1. Identify three reasons why students could be bored in school.
2. Discuss the importance of engaging students in their own learning.
3. List five classroom activities/projects designed to engage students.
4. How would you incorporate cooperative learning activities in your classroom?
5. Define *relevance*.
    - Why is relevance such an important consideration in planning instruction?
    - What indicators are used in determining if instruction is relevant to students' learning?
    - How do you evaluate to determine if instruction is relevant?

# 9

# CREATING A POSITIVE SCHOOL CULTURE

> The relationship among the adults in the schoolhouse has more impact on the quality and character of the schoolhouse—and the accomplishments of youngsters—more than any other factor.
>
> —Ronald Barth, 2001

How many times have you visited a school and were quickly able to determine the type of environment that existed? Were you recognized and greeted with respect by school staff? Was there a sense of good feeling among the students and teachers? Was the physical condition of the building conducive to learning? Was the building itself clean and well kept? Did students seem well behaved in the hallways, classrooms, and lunchroom, as well as outside on the playground?

The school *climate* can be easily determined soon after one enters the building. *Where* students learn is as important as *how* they learn and *what* they learn. Students spend most of their waking hours in school. The atmosphere existing within the school impacts the quality of learning and achievement that occurs.

School *culture* refers to the values, beliefs, practices, expectations, attitudes, traditions, behaviors, and procedures that make up the personality of the school. These build up over time as teachers, students, parents, and administrators work together to deal with challenges, solve problems, and when necessary, cope with failure. School culture develops over a period of time.

Just as an individual's personality develops, so does the culture of the school. School culture refers to the history of the school. It is the day-to-day experiences that have taken place over time. School climate refers to the present time—the perceptions and behaviors currently being demonstrated. Simply defined, school culture is the way the school does business, making clear what is important and what is not!

Every school has a culture, whether or not the staff is attentive to it or helps shape it. The principal, being the leader of the school, makes a difference in the development of the culture within the building. It is the responsibility of the principal to implement strategies that create, maintain, and/or improve the culture.

Learning takes place best in a positive environment—or positive school culture. A positive school culture will produce more student and teacher success than any other type of school improvement effort currently, or formerly, being implemented. School cultures can be thought of as being on a continuum ranging from *bureaucratic* to *collegial*. There is also one additional type of school culture, known as a *toxic* culture. Schools demonstrating this type of school culture traditionally have frequent teacher turnover, as well as having a negative climate within the school itself.

## THE IMPORTANCE OF PRINCIPAL-TEACHER RELATIONSHIPS IN THE SCHOOL SETTING

How principals and teachers relate to one another differs greatly among schools. This occurs because some teachers see principals as facilitators, supporters, and reinforcers rather than leaders, directors, and guiders. (E. McEwan, *Seven Steps to Effective Instructional Leadership*. Thousand Oaks, CA: Corwin Press, 2003).

The principal occupies an important position in the school. As leader of a team of professionals, as well as classified employees, he or she establishes important relationships with the staff. Principals have the ability to improve teacher perceptions by establishing quality relationships among and between staff members.

In every school, both principals and teachers alike have to deal with issues such as student discipline. Although the principal is continually involved with working with student discipline problems, his or her role is different than that of the teacher. However, in many situations the principal and the teacher work together as a team on major discipline issues. Therefore, it becomes important for principals and teachers to work together for purposes of providing mutual support. One indicator of successful teachers is a positive relationship developed with their principals, which can motivate them to do their very best work.

# EXAMPLES OF DIFFERENT TYPES OF SCHOOL CULTURES

Characteristics of a *collegial* school culture include

- High expectations of students and staff
- Open communications between and among students and staff
- Collaborative behavior
- Caring attitude among all those in the school building
- Appreciation and recognition of the importance of learning
- Trust and confidence among students and staff members
- Caring, celebration of success, and humor
- Focus on student engagement in their own learning
- Collegiality
- Traditions (the rituals, ceremonies, and symbols that strengthen the school culture)
- Group involvement in decision making
- Tangible support for one another

(J. Saphier and M. King, "Good Seeds Grow in Strong Cultures: Student Learning Grows in Professional Cultures," *Educational Leadership*, 42, no. 6, March 1985, pp. 67–74)

Collegial school culture demonstrates a feeling of togetherness and collaboration. Sharing of ideas and resources is a daily activity. Solving problems involves teachers, parents, and administrators. Involving students is not unusual in this type of school culture.

Characteristics of a *bureaucratic* school culture include:

- Principal is at the helm; teachers are followers of the dictated regimen.
- Strong emphasis on standardization or following the book.
- Teachers work in isolation with little chance for interaction with colleagues.
- Policies and procedures are mandated from above with little or no input from teachers.

In a bureaucratic-type school culture, many teachers feel isolated with little opportunity to contribute. Little incentive to grow professionally exists. Teachers are encouraged to solve problems within their own classrooms. Principals and parents are involved only when the teachers are unable to solve the problem on their own.

Characteristics of a *toxic* school culture include:

- Students viewed as the problem rather than as valued clients
- Believe they are doing the best they can and don't search out new ideas
- Frequently share stories about the history of the school that are often negative or discouraging
- Rarely share ideas, materials, or solutions to classroom problems
- Have few ceremonies or school traditions that celebrate what is good and hopeful about their workplace.

(T. D. Deal and K. D. Peterson, *Shaping School Culture: The Heart of Leadership*. San Francisco: Jossey-Bass, 1998)

Signs to watch for in your school that identify an *unhealthy* school culture:

- Discipline is punitive, not constructive in nature.
- Little collaboration among staff.
- Resistance to change.
- Staff takes little responsibility for student achievement.
- Engaging students in their own learning is not a priority.
- Little involvement of parents in the school program.

The school culture has a direct impact on teachers. It can affect the way teachers relate to each other, to their students, to parents, and to administrators. It can even affect how teachers work with the community.

Creating and sustaining the culture of the school is the responsibility of all those who work there. The choices that are made will determine the type of school culture that develops. This is a challenge in which every teacher needs to become involved as part of his or her daily responsibility.

The goal of every school should be to work toward creating a positive culture. The reasons are obvious:

- The school becomes a home away from home. Who wants their home to project a negative and uncaring atmosphere?
- Student achievement is a priority for all teachers and administrators. Learning occurs best in a positive environment.
- The mental health of the entire staff is enhanced when working in a collegial workplace.
- Schools need to be characterized as being successful. This happens best in a positive environment.

- A school can become a model of positive school culture for other schools in the area. It is catching!

## DISCUSSION QUESTIONS

1. What type of school culture exists in your school or in a school you attended? Identify specific evidence to support your choice.
2. How does an unhealthy school culture impact student achievement?
3. Do you see any aspects of your school or school district that need to be changed in order to create a healthier school climate?
4. Discuss contributions teachers can make to improve or sustain the existing culture in their school.
5. What role do students play in creating school culture?

# 10

# THE EFFECT OF POVERTY ON TEACHING AND LEARNING

> Poverty must not be a bar to learning, and learning must offer an escape from poverty.
>
> —Lyndon B. Johnson

Increasing numbers of our nation's children are living in poverty. These children are coming into our schools having needs related to living under these circumstances. Poverty can put students at risk and create special challenges for them in the school environment. For the purpose of definition, the term *at risk* refers to students who are likely to fail in school or in life due to their social circumstances. It does not appear that any single factor places a child at risk. Rather, when more than one factor is present, there is a compounding effect, and the likelihood for failure increases significantly.

Poverty is considered a major risk factor. Other factors contributing to placing a child at risk for academic failure include but are not limited to the following:

- Having very young, single parents
- Low educational level of parents
- Abuse and/or neglect
- Substance abuse
- Living in dangerous neighborhoods
- Homelessness
- Mobility
- Exposure to limited or inappropriate educational experiences

The increase in the number of children living in poverty contributes to the diversity in our classrooms. This results in making both teaching and learning more challenging. Teachers and principals must become knowledgeable and sensitive to the social and educational needs of those children living in poverty. Doing so means seeking support from others and participating in relevant professional development activities, including formal college training opportunities.

Identifying students who are at risk is often difficult due to class size. Such situations can make it harder for teachers to determine which students in the class are at risk. Warning signs that at risk children may exhibit include the following:

- poor academic grades and achievement
- delay in language development
- delay in reading development
- aggressiveness
- violence
- social withdrawal
- poor attendance
- depression
- failing to complete assignments
- poor study habits
- inability to concentrate or focus on task at hand
- not interacting well with others
- poor appearance and/or poor hygiene

Teachers must be attentive to the warning signs that identify students who are living in poverty and are considered as being at risk. The needs of these students must be kept in mind when developing classroom management procedures and writing lesson plans. Diversity presents the opportunity for teachers to improve the quality of education for all students and at the same time provide a variety of learning activities. As our schools become more diverse, the need for understanding and accepting differences becomes a major focus for teachers as well as other school personnel.

When considering the nature of at risk students, all impacting factors should be taken into consideration. Education takes place both inside and outside school. Schools are only one of many social institutions that educate, or fail to educate, students at risk. In addition to the school, the family and the community are vital educating institutions in our society. In summary, young people are at risk if they have been in contact with inadequate or inappropriate educational experiences in the family, community, or school. The concern is how one goes about determining which experiences would be labeled as either inadequate or inappropriate—or both.

## THE URBAN SCHOOL SETTING: SOCIAL CONDITIONS AND HARDSHIPS AFFECTING SUCCESS OF STUDENTS

*Concentration of Poverty*

Few dispute that urban school districts are confronted with multiple challenges. The isolation of urban neighborhoods, concentrated poverty, and the possibility of family instability all contribute to severe conditions and risks of failure in the urban schools. These issues are further magnified in the schools when teachers are not adequately prepared for this type of school environment, lack cultural sensitivity and awareness, and use pedagogical methodologies that are not culturally congruent. Although there are occasions of impressive educational success, the vast majority of urban schools continue to face inequalities that impact learning and achievement. (J. Kozol, *Savage Inequalities*. New York: HarperCollins, 1991)

Concentrated poverty is often noted as the biggest challenge facing urban schools. Poverty can also influence a child's perceptions, interactions, and relationships. (M. Haberman, "Who Benefits from Failing Urban School Districts?" http://www.habermanfoundation.org/Articles/Default.aspx?id=06, March 2003) Urban children affected by living in concentrated poverty may

- experience difficulty trusting adults
- avoid interacting with others
- demonstrate feelings of hopelessness
- reveal as little as possible about themselves
- respond only by giving and taking orders

One out of every four American children, about 14 million, attend an urban district school. (M. Haberman, *Who Benefits from Failing Urban School Districts?* Haberman Educational Foundation, 2003) http://www.habermanfoundation.org/Articles/Default.aspx?id=06) The U. S. Census Bureau (2005) reported that 37 million people (12.7 percent) were living in poverty. The effects of family poverty are more severe when there is a high concentration of low-income families and individuals living in the neighborhood. The result often is that depressed attitudes and motivation may be accepted as normative, thereby reducing urban children's expectations and hope for the future, including success in school. (L. Simons, R. Conger, and G. Brody, "Collective Socialization and Child Conduct Problems," *Youth and Society*, 2004, pp. 267–92)

*Violence*

Schools should be safe havens where the environment is focused on teaching and learning. The impact of violence in urban neighborhoods and within the family structure inhibits both the academic and social development of urban children and places them at particular risk of victimization. (M. Schwab-Stone, C. Chen, E. Greenberger, D. Silver, J. Lichtman, and C. Voyce, "The Effects of Violence Exposure on Urban Youth," *Journal of the American Academy of Child and Adolescent Psychiatry*, 1991, pp. 359–67) Many of these children are harmed, both emotionally and physically, within their own homes and neighborhoods. For many of these children, violence has become an integral part of their lives. Violent behavior is often accepted and has become the norm among family and peer groups in some communities.

Because of the constant violence that surrounds urban children, many frequently act out their hostility and frustration by being disruptive in the classroom. Frustration and depression are common feelings of both adults and children who live in depressed areas and witness violence. This frustration level may present itself in some form of aggression, which may be expressed as violence toward self or others. It can take the form of passive resistance, where students lose their sense of hope, will, and self. When urban children are distracted because they are anticipating violence or danger, this fear may cause them to experience difficulty in learning and staying focused in school. If this becomes a regular occurrence, they can become academically discouraged and more likely to fail at school. (M. Haberman, *Who Benefits from Failing Urban School Districts?* http://www.habermanfoundation.org/Articles/Default.aspx?id=06, March 2003)

## FOCUSING ON THE NATURE AND TYPE OF INSTRUCTION IN URBAN SCHOOLS

The level of student achievement is based on success in the classroom. That being true, ongoing urban teaching includes cultural references and takes into account the social conditions and hardships that many urban students experience. When teachers use students' cultural and social experiences as a means to implement best practices and to develop new knowledge, learning becomes significant. (Y. Pardon, H. Waxman, and H. Rivera, "Educating Hispanic Students: Effective Instructional Practices." www.cal.org/cred/Pubs/PracBrief5.html, 2002)

When urban teachers understand resiliency in students, support behaviors that demonstrate high expectations, consider social dynamics, and use diverse teaching methods, student success is inevitable. (H. Mehan and I. Villanueva, "Forming Academic Identities: Accommodation without Assimilation among Involuntary Minorities," *Anthropology and Education Quarterly* 1994, pp. 91–117) Effective teaching strategies should include, but not be limited to, providing relevant learning activities and allowing for classroom discussions and dialogue between and among students.

Teachers who embrace a multicultural philosophy and have proven success in working in diverse classrooms can be referred to as "culturally responsive." These five specific characteristics define a culturally responsive teacher:

- Has knowledge of the complex nature of ethnicity
- Has knowledge of stages of cultural identity
- Has ability to function in a multicultural environment
- Demonstrates democratic attitudes and values
- Has the ability to view society from a multiethnic viewpoint

(J. A. Banks, *Cultural Diversity and Education*. Boston, MA: Allyn and Bacon, 2001)

Students attending urban high-poverty schools face many challenges, including concentrated poverty, violence, victimization, and often family instability. The impact of these social conditions and hardships can be brought into the classrooms. However, research tells us that effective teachers within the urban schools can help overcome these obstacles and help students experience both social and academic success. (M. Haberman, *Who Benefits from Failing Urban School Districts?* http://www.habermanfoundation.org/Articles/Default.aspx?id=06, March 2003) Poverty does affect teaching and learning, but dedicated, culturally responsive teachers can turn things around and provide opportunities for student achievement in schools where poverty does exist.

## DISCUSSION QUESTIONS

1. Discuss ways you would plan instruction to meet the needs of at risk students in your classroom.

2. In what ways can at risk students be motivated?
3. Identify social conditions that students living in poverty have brought into your classroom or that you have observed in other classrooms.
4. What conditions have to exist for a teacher to become culturally responsive?
5. What are some ways a school can accommodate students living in poverty?

## 11

# TIME FOR REFLECTION

## Putting Your Thoughts into Writing

As stated in the introduction, the purpose of this book is to inform and educate. Keeping that in mind, it is now time for reflection.

The reader is asked to react to the following questions by reflecting on his or her own personal and professional circumstances. The reader can respond in one of the following ways: (1) as being actively engaged in teaching at the present time, (2) using experiences or observations from other classrooms, or (3) projecting feelings focusing on the time you will be actively engaged in teaching.

Space will be provided to record your reflections. Often when thoughts are put into writing, the result can be more impacting.

1. What specific techniques or instructional practices have you found to be successful in terms of engaging students in their own learning?

2. How do you work with students who resist, one way or another, becoming engaged in their own learning?

3. How important do you feel people skills are in terms of making a difference in being successful in the classroom?

4. Reviewing the people skills discussed in chapter 2, identify three that describe you best. Support your choices with evidence.

5. "Inadequate people skills lead to inadequate teaching performance in the classroom." React to this statement.

6. Discuss your reaction to completing the self-assessment activity in chapter 2.

7. What do you see as the differences between a job and a professional position such as teaching?

8. What impact does your classroom management plan have on your day-to-day teaching?

9. Did you find any of the models of classroom management plans relevant or helpful to you?

10. What activities, programs, or procedures do you find successful when working with parents?

11. How do you involve parents who have limited time to become active in their child's schooling?

12. Most teachers must deal with uncooperative or even hostile parents. Identify a situation in which you had to deal with such a parent and explain how you handled it. Include the outcome.

13. In chapter 6, a survey was presented. It asked those responding to identify teacher traits in one of two ways: as a people skill or as an academic skill. React to the results of this survey.

14. Classrooms today present many challenges to teachers. Identify three challenges you have experienced.

15. In chapter 8, cooperative learning was presented as an example of how to engage students in their own learning. Have you used this teaching method in your classroom? Do you see it as a possibility if you have not? If not, why not?

16. "Creating a positive school culture contributes to students' achievement." Discuss your thoughts on this statement.

17. What climate, also known as school culture, exists in your school? Support your answer with evidence.

18. What can an individual teacher do to contribute to improving or maintaining the climate that exists in his or her school?

19. Instructionally, how do you provide for at risk students in your classroom?

20. Children living in poverty are increasing in numbers both in society and in the classroom. What accommodations do you provide for these students to help them feel comfortable in the school setting and at the same time help them achieve academically?

21. How does a teacher become culturally responsive in today's diverse classrooms? What resources are available to support teachers in this situation?

22. How important is the physical arrangement of your classroom? Identify how arranging classroom furniture, technology, and resources creates the opportunity for better classroom management and for learning.

23. How do you integrate the use of technology into your instructional program? Cite examples.

24. In chapter 3, several print-to-practice teaching strategies were presented for implementation in your classroom. Of the strategies listed, identify those you feel could be helpful to you.

25. Describe a model classroom in which students could achieve to their highest potential.

## 12

# SUMMARY AND CONCLUSION

### PRIORITY SCHOOLS: WHAT WORKS TO IMPROVE STUDENT ACHIEVEMENT?

*At the school level*

- Guaranteed and viable curriculum
- Challenging goals and effective feedback
- Parent and community involvement
- Safe and orderly environment
- Collegiality and professionalism

*At the teacher level*

- Instructional strategies
- Classroom management
- Classroom curriculum and design
- People skills

*At the student level*

- Home environment
- Learned intelligence and background knowledge
- Motivation

(Robert Marzano, *What Works in Schools: Translating Research into Action.* Alexandria, VA: Association for Supervision and Curriculum Development, 2003)

Teaching is an essential profession. It would be difficult to find many people who would disagree with that statement. Of course, there would be some who would say they had several unpleasant memories related to their school experience. So be it. The reality is that teaching is here to stay!

The nature of teaching continues to change. Teaching must change to meet the needs of society, which also is changing—sometimes with alarming speed. Societal changes have a tremendous impact on the nature of teaching.

There are at least three schools of thought regarding the nature of change. Some look at change as being good and necessary. They support their opinion with a strong rationale. Others question the need for or outcome of change. Others express more neutral thinking. They question whether change is sometimes made just for the sake of change, or to keep up with current times. It actually does not matter which school of thought one subscribes to—change is inevitable!

Change occurs on a regular basis in teaching. Schools reflect the changing society in which they exist. Society will continue to change, and therefore schools must change accordingly. We all understand that change is based on needs. Education must meet the needs of students. Decades of change in society have impacted the nature of teaching. As the nature of teaching has been impacted, the role and responsibilities of teachers have also been impacted.

The meaning of effective teaching and the effective teacher has been redefined. At one time, teachers had two major responsibilities. One was to be academically prepared in their content area; the other was to teach that content to their students.

Changes in society have added responsibilities and expectations of those teaching in today's schools. Of course, teachers are still required to be academically prepared and to teach content to their students.

Teachers continue to act *in loco parentis,* being the daytime parent for students. Performing that role has become more complex and complicated. Acts of student misbehavior have become more problematic and serious in nature. Parental support and involvement is not evident in some schools. Teachers now work with many students from nontraditional families, as compared to the past when the traditional family was the norm.

The nature of teaching includes changes in curriculum and instruction. The introduction of technology into the classroom is one example that required teachers to update their knowledge and teaching skills. Another example impacting the nature of teaching is working in a more culturally diverse classroom. These changes create new challenges for teachers. Being an effective teacher in today's schools takes on a new definition.

Interpersonal or people skills have always been an integral part of teaching. Students are bringing many serious and complicated challenges into the schools, and teachers must deal with them.

How important are people skills? A vast number of teachers leaving the profession within three to five years do so because of their inadequate classroom management skills. Managing people plays a major role in determining success in the classroom. The question is, can a teacher's people skills be improved? Given appropriate support and time, the results could be positive.

Good teachers are both academically prepared and demonstrate effective people skills. Being academically prepared involves more than knowing your subject matter. It involves creating a classroom management plan, writing good lesson plans, and implementing instructional strategies that work.

The classroom management plan provides the blueprint for success in the classroom. It must be individual to the teacher creating it. This plan must focus on both instruction and behavioral management, while at the same time considering student engagement. The classroom management plan is only a plan. If necessary, it can be revised or totally rewritten. The plan should be reflective of the philosophy and style of the teacher.

Once a classroom management plan is in place, the next task is writing good lesson plans. As stated, the classroom management plan provides the blueprint for the instructional program. Lesson plans need to follow that blueprint.

Planning for teaching is essential. Proper planning translates into successful teaching. Lesson plans provide the tool for such planning. Guidelines for writing lesson plans were presented in chapter 1. Writing good lesson plans is a learned skill that tends to improve with experience.

One of the most critical components of a lesson plan is the instructional strategies. Chapter 3 included several print-to-practice strategies that work. Instructional strategies bring the lesson plan to life in the classroom.

Having a positive mind-set is extremely important. Starting each day with a good attitude sets the tone for the entire day. Another important strategy is to set high expectations for behavior in the classroom and being proactive while doing so. Let students know that misbehavior will result in specific consequences.

Using a variety of instructional methods and activities will increase the probability of engaging students and keeping them focused.

Students spend most of their waking hours each day at school. Creating a friendly and inviting atmosphere in the classroom is very important. It is a plus toward motivating students!

Providing a successful experience for students at school should include working with parents—namely, establishing a home-school connection. The importance of including parents in their children's education cannot be overemphasized. Children of all ages and grade levels want their parents to be aware of what they are doing at school. Working with parents is an important responsibility of the classroom teacher. Technology provides an additional opportunity for communicating with parents that was not available only a few decades ago.

Using surveys was discussed in chapter 6. Surveys elicit opinions from responders. These opinions provide data for various purposes. Surveys presented in chapter 6 were related to effective teachers and teaching. Of interest was data from one particular survey indicating people skills as being monumentally important toward being successful in the classroom.

Of course, it is important to keep in mind that many surveys create data based upon opinions, not facts. The results are still worth studying, as they reflect opinions that may be of value.

Teachers are challenged on a regular basis. These challenges range in nature from simple to complex. More complex challenges include dealing with violence, bullying, and the presence of gang affiliation. Chapter 7 discussed types of school violence.

Schools must deal with these challenges by providing intervention programs aimed at curbing violent behavior. Additional opportunities must be made available for teachers, as well as other staff members, focusing on how to recognize risk factors associated with such behavior.

The nature of teaching has changed dramatically. Meeting the increasing number of serious challenges in schools has been partly responsible for such change. Survival in the classroom is a major issue.

Teaching can be both difficult and demanding. Students bring enormous challenges into the school. Schools do not create problems but must find solutions to them. Teachers are instrumental in this endeavor. However, considering all the facts, teaching continues to be the most essential profession. Who can plan on having a successful future without the support of good teachers?

Teaching continues to teach all other professions. The influence of teachers touches everyone, in one way or another. A major responsibility of teachers has always been, and continues to be, the teaching of subject matter. To be successful in the classroom today, as in the past, teachers must be academically prepared.

Having effective people skills is critical in today's changing classrooms. The expectations and responsibilities society has placed on teachers in today's schools are increasing on a regular basis.

A continuing concern is the number of teachers leaving the profession early in their careers. Recruiting good teachers has always been a major responsibility of school districts across the country. Retaining good teachers is equally, if not more, important.

The following are just a few activities that can support the retaining of good teachers:

- Teacher training programs at the college level should provide students with earlier hands-on opportunities in schools. Waiting until the junior or senior year for in-school experiences can be too late.
- School districts can provide entry-level, year-long teacher induction programs. These programs should begin prior to the opening of the school year and include ongoing activities.
- Each school can provide opportunities for inexperienced teachers to observe successful teachers in action.
- Schools can develop teams within the building. The team should include a new teacher and an experienced teacher.
- School districts can offer professional development activities geared to the needs of beginning or inexperienced teachers.

Getting it done in the classroom requires many skills. Two of the most important are: (1) using instructional strategies that have a positive effect on the level of student achievement; and (2) possessing and demonstrating appropriate people or interpersonal skills necessary for managing a classroom successfully on a regular basis.

Several important print-to-practice strategies were identified. Of course, these are just a few of the many strategies that contribute to effective instruction. Each class of students has a personality. Teachers must adjust instruction to the needs of students in each class they teach. Good teachers have the skills necessary to do this.

Effective instruction does not just happen! Teachers must be academically prepared in their subject matter content. Good teachers are lifelong learners. They take advantage of a variety of learning experiences such as participating in professional development opportunities.

Knowing subject matter content alone does not make a teacher effective in the classroom. In order to deliver content, teachers must have those interpersonal or people skills necessary to successfully manage students in the classroom. Teaching is about working with people!

Chapter 2 included an opportunity for the reader to reflect on his or her own people skills through use of self-evaluation. People skills, like academic skills, can be improved. First, one must realize that certain people skills need improvement. Next, one must determine what type of support is available to assist in the process of working toward such improvement. Improving interpersonal skills can be more difficult than increasing academic expertise! However, with appropriate support, time, and effort, it can be done.

Other than the words *mother* and *father*, *teacher* is the most important word in our vocabulary! To teach is to learn. To witness a student grasping a new concept or idea is what teaching is all about. It is about guiding the lives of young people—preparing them for what lies ahead. Everyone has been influenced by a good teacher somewhere along his or her educational journey. Teaching must be both fun and exciting, whether you are working with preschoolers learning their ABCs or with high school seniors learning calculus or chemistry! From start to finish of their educational journey, students are in the hands of their teachers.

## THE IMPORTANCE OF PROFESSIONAL DEVELOPMENT AND LIFELONG LEARNING

Participating in professional development is one way of increasing the professional skills you already possess. It is a process of continuous improvement and the refining of your teaching potential. It is also about goal setting. All educators need to take advantage of professional development, such as taking a college course or attending workshops or conferences. Professional development activities can be short-term or long-term in duration. Positive thinking goes along with professional development: if you think you can be better, then you can be! Being positive and setting realistic goals will keep you motivated to improve your professional career. Teaching is about lifelong learning experiences, which includes participating in continuous professional development programs and activities.

# INDEX

academic preparation, 12
at-risk students, 102, 104
attitude, 19

behavioral expectations, 40
body language, 33–34
boredom, 88
bullying, 81–83
bureaucratic school culture, 84

"Caught Being Good," 44
challenges, types of, 75–76
change, nature of, 119
child abuse, 83–85
classroom: changes in, 46;
    environment, 43–44; physical
    arrangement of, 39; rules, 45–46;
    student–centered, 92–94
classroom management plan, 48–49,
    120; definition of, 36, 48; flexibility
    of, 50; guidelines, 49–50; key
    points, 37; models, 50–56
collegial school culture, 83
common sense, 27–28
communication skills, 18
cooperative learning, 90–92

Davis, Ruth, xii
discussion questions, 21, 35, 47, 56,
    63, 74, 86, 95, 101, 108

diversity, 43

Einstein, Albert, x
engaging students, 88–89; first day of
    school, 40; gangs in schools, 85

Home-School Connection, 57–58

Johnson, Lawrence J., xi

Kennedy, John F., ix

Lesson planning, 10–11, 121;
    guidelines for, 10; quality of, 11
listening skills, 25
*loco parentis*, 9, 119–120

misbehavior, consequences of, 44–45

new school year, 38–39

parent involvement, 58–59, 60–61;
    communicating with, 62
people skills, 24–35, 120
positive mind set, 37–38
positive school culture, 82
poverty: children living in, 102;
    definition of, 102; factors
    contributing to, 102–103; warning
    signs, 103

principal-teacher relationships, 97–98
"print-to-practice strategies," 37–46
professional development, 124–125

Questioning, as a teaching strategy, 18

Rather, Dan xi
reteaching, 34–35

school climate, 96
school culture: bureaucratic, 99; collegial, 98; positive, 96–97, 100; toxic, 99; unhealthy, 99–100
self-confidence, 26
sense of humor, 19, 27
Shaw, George Bernard, xi
standardized test scores, 21
standards, 40–41
students: behavior, 36–37, 41–42; engaging, 16–17; praising, 17–18; self-assessment, 11
student teaching, 14–15
surveys: analysis of, 72–73; best and worst teachers, 67; purpose of, 64

teachers: approachable, 20; classroom management skills, 15–16; effective, 10–11; high performing, 11; responsibilities of, 11; retaining, 123
teaching: effective, 1–24; nature of, 15–16; planning for, 10; service profession, 9; team player, 19–20; ten commandments of, 15–16; variety of, 42
technology, classroom use, 20
time management skills, 19

urban school setting: nature and type of instruction, 106–107; social conditions, 104–106

violence, 76;; examining, 78–79; in schools, 76; in urban schools, 105–106; preventing, 76–77; risk factors, 77–78

Ward, William A., ix
Wong, Harry & Rosemary, 28

# ABOUT THE AUTHOR

**Jerry H. Boyle** has spent several decades as a professional educator. He began his career as an elementary teacher in a suburban school district near Cincinnati, Ohio. He received his bachelor's degree in secondary education and his master's degree in educational administration/elementary education from the University of Cincinnati. He began his administrative career as an assistant elementary principal, followed by promotion to the position of elementary principal, in one of the largest schools in the greater Cincinnati area. In 1979, he received his doctorate in educational administration from the University of Cincinnati. For the next two decades he served as an elementary principal in Cincinnati public schools, during which time he was asked to assume additional responsibilities as a lead principal.

Dr. Boyle's professional experiences include serving as the executive director of the Mayerson Academy, a nationally known training facility for professional educators in the greater Cincinnati area. While serving in this position, he taught part-time at the University of Cincinnati's Graduate School of Education. His expertise is in the area of curriculum and instruction.

This book is a reflection of both Dr. Boyle's academic training and educational experiences. His comprehensive background contributes to the content of this book. His extensive knowledge, through performance and observation, of what makes an effective teacher is based upon those experiences.

# ACKNOWLEDGMENTS

My wife *Mary*, my son *Jay* & my daughter *Jill* for supporting my first attempt at writing a book.

*Suzanne Bender*, who was always there to help me with ongoing technology issues.

*Craig Braun*, who consistently kept me on course when I tended to slow down.

*Dr. Lawrence Johnson*, who contributed the inspired Foreword for the book.

*Dr. Larry Rowedder*, whose advice served as support for my writing.

*Gwen Walton*, who took time to assess my writing.

*Kathleen Ware*, who took time to evaluate my writing skills in general.

*Kathy Witherop*, who contributed her expertise to the format of the book.

All of the outstanding *educators* that have inspired me during my professional career, especially *Elsie Minnick* and *Harold Maddux*, who believed in me at the start!

The thousands of *students* and *parents* that I had the pleasure of working with throughout the years.